W0018780

2

TIME ZONES
WORKBOOK | THIRD EDITION

CARMELLA LIESKE

NATIONAL GEOGRAPHIC
LEARNING

Australia · Brazil · Mexico · Singapore · United Kingdom · United States

National Geographic Learning,
a Cengage Company

Time Zones Workbook 2 Third Edition
Carmella Lieske

Publisher: Andrew Robinson

Managing Editor: Derek Mackrell

Editorial Assistant: Elaine Lum

Additional Editorial Support: Sarah Jane Lewis

Director of Global Marketing: Ian Martin

Senior Product Marketing Manager: Anders Bylund

Heads of Regional Marketing:
    Charlotte Ellis (Europe, Middle East and Africa)
    Kiel Hamm (Asia)
    Irina Pereyra (Latin America)

Senior Production Controller: Tan Jin Hock

Associate Media Researcher: Jeffrey Millies

Senior Designer: Lisa Trager

Operations Support: Rebecca G. Barbush,
    Hayley Chwazik-Gee

Manufacturing Planner: Mary Beth Hennebury

Composition: Symmetry Creative Production, Inc.

© 2021 Cengage Learning, Inc.

ALL RIGHTS RESERVED. No part of this work covered by the copyright herein may be reproduced or distributed in any form or by any means, except as permitted by U.S. copyright law, without the prior written permission of the copyright owner.

"National Geographic", "National Geographic Society" and the Yellow Border Design are registered trademarks of the National Geographic Society ® Marcas Registradas

For permission to use material from this text or product,
submit all requests online at **cengage.com/permissions**
Further permissions questions can be emailed to
permissionrequest@cengage.com

ISBN-13: 978-0-357-42638-8

National Geographic Learning
200 Pier 4 Boulevard
Boston, MA 02210
USA

Locate your local office at **international.cengage.com/region**

Visit National Geographic Learning online at **ELTNGL.com**
Visit our corporate website at **www.cengage.com**

Printed in the United States of America
Print Number: 05 Print Year: 2021

CONTENTS

1

WHAT DO YOU LIKE TO DO?

PREVIEW

A **Unscramble the words.**

1 r u g i t a   g u i t a r

2 d w r a   ___ ___a___ ___ ___

3 o c e e k y c i h   ___ ___ ___ ___   ___ ___ ___ ___ ___ y

4 o k e o b m i o c s   ___ ___ ___ ___ c ___   ___ ___ o ___ ___

5 r a i o m i g   ___ ___ ___ g ___ ___ ___

6 a t o l v l e b y l   ___ ___ l ___ ___ ___ ___ ___ ___

7 n e s i n t   ___ ___ ___ ___ s ___

8 a r e t k a   ___ a ___ ___ ___ ___

B **Write.** Use the words from **A**.

1 play ___the guitar___, _____, _____, _____

2 do _____, _____

3 collect _____

4 _____ with pencils

C **Write.** What are some hobbies you would like to start?

_____

_____

LANGUAGE FOCUS

A **Complete the conversation.** Circle the correct answers.

Dave: Hi, Jamie. [1] **When** / **What** do you like to do after school?

Jamie: I like to [2] **draw** / **draws**.

Dave: [3] **How many** / **How often** do you do it?

Jamie: After school every day. How about you? What do you [4] **like to do** / **like do** after school?

Dave: I play soccer [5] **four** / **fourth** times a week. Do you [6] **like to** / **like** play soccer?

Jamie: Yes, I do. I really like [7] **to play** / **play** soccer! My team practices [8] **to** / **before** school. Let's play together! We meet at 6:30 on Tuesday mornings.

Dave: Um, that's too early for me.

B **Complete the conversations.** Add one missing word to each line.

1 **Lucas:** What do you like to do ~~on~~ weekends?

    Anna: I like to go the park.

2 **Tammy:** When you do karate?

    Diego: I do it twice a week Tuesdays and Saturdays.

3 **Ben:** Do you like collect comic books?

    Jenny: No, but I like read them.

4 **David:** How often do you play piano?

    Kevin: I play it three a week.

5 **Zoe:** Do you like to origami?

    Ian: Yes, do.

6 **Emily:** How do you exercise?

    Olivia: I exercise once week on Sundays.

C **Match.** Join the two parts of the conversation.

1 Hi, Susana. Do you like to play sports? ○   ○ **a** I play the piano. And I can sing, too.

2 Yeah? What instruments do you play? ○   ○ **b** Sure! I have lots of superhero comic books.

3 Cool! What other things do you like to do? ○   ○ **c** Well, I like to collect comic books.

4 Really? Me, too! Can I see your collection? ○   ○ **d** Hey, Peter. Mmm, no, but I like to play music.

WORKING WITH GAMES

As a child, J. T. Smith played lots of board games. Now, he's an adult, but he still likes to play games!

J. T. made his hobby into his business. He started a very successful company called "the Game Crafter." It helps people make their own board or card games.

On the Game Crafter website, people design their own games. The Game Crafter then makes them. It sells them, too! Sometimes big toy companies buy the games and sell them in stores around the world.

You can make your own game, too! Does it sound difficult? You can practice and improve your ideas. Make your hobby into your job, and your job can be fun!

A **Read the article.** Circle **T** for True, **F** for False, or **NG** for Not Given.

1 J. T. Smith is a child.   **T**   **F**   **NG**

2 J. T.'s work started as his hobby.   **T**   **F**   **NG**

3 The Game Crafter helps people make their own board games.   **T**   **F**   **NG**

4 The Game Crafter sells the games online.   **T**   **F**   **NG**

5 J. T. says that everyone should make their own board games.   **T**   **F**   **NG**

B **Look at the hobbies below.** Do you think people can make money from them?

READING

A Read the information in the box. What does it tell us? Check (✓) your answers.

☐ where gorillas live   ☐ why gorillas die   ☐ what gorillas eat

SAVING THE MOUNTAIN GORILLAS

There are only about 1,000 mountain gorillas left in the wild. Addison Barrett (Addy) read about this and wanted to help save them. Her dream was to get everyone excited about gorillas, so she started a blog called *Gorilla Heroes*. She
5 teaches people about gorillas and posts information about her projects. Even though Addy was only seven years old when she started the blog, she had many excellent ideas.

For one of Addy's projects, young people wrote short stories and poems about endangered animals (animals that
10 are few in number). Addy also had the idea of the #GorillaPie Challenge. To do the challenge, you get a friend to throw a whipped cream pie at you. You film this and share the video with friends. Then, you give money to help save the gorillas, and you get your friends to do the
15 challenge as well! If someone gives $100 or more, Addy and her family will throw a pie at themselves! In 2019, her projects collected more than $6,000 to help the gorillas!

Mountain Gorillas
• live in forests high in the mountains
• only found in Rwanda, Democratic Republic of Congo, and Uganda
Problems for Mountain Gorillas
• people spread diseases to them
• forests are getting smaller
• killed for food

Addy started a blog about gorillas when she was seven years old.

B EXAM PRACTICE Answer the questions about *Saving the Mountain Gorillas*.

1 MAIN IDEA What's the article about?

   a taking care of sick mountain gorillas

   b getting people to care about mountain gorillas

   c building new homes for mountain gorillas

2 VOCABULARY In line 1, *left in the wild* means _____ .

   a going to the zoo   b living in natural areas   c living in homes as pets

3 INFERENCE The *Gorilla Heroes* blog is LEAST likely to have _____ .

   a information about Addy's favorite books

   b poems about endangered animals

   c information about the #GorillaPie Challenge

4 DETAIL For the #GorillaPie Challenge, people _____ .

    a sold pies

    b fed pies to gorillas

    c threw pies at their friends

5 INFERENCE What does Addy's family most likely think about the #GorillaPie Challenge?

    a They support it.

    b They think it's a bad idea.

    c They don't know about it.

C Answer the questions.

    1 What do you want to inspire others to care about?

    _____

    2 Does your school have a group to help endangered animals?

    _____

VOCABULARY

A Complete the sentences. Use the words in the box.

improve	practices	take a break	excellent	talent	expert

    1 This town is a(n) _____ place to live—it's quiet and the people are friendly.

    2 She's a wildlife _____—she knows a lot about animals.

    3 She has amazing writing _____—her books often win prizes.

    4 My school's baseball team _____ three times a week.

    5 I'm tired. Let's _____ .

    6 Reading is a good way to _____ your language skills.

B Complete the sentences. Circle the correct answers.

    1 My mom found a hole in her new backpack, so she took it **back / away** to the store.

    2 My dad takes me **out / down** for pizza once a month.

    3 The famous ice hockey player Wayne Gretzky took **in / up** ice hockey when he was two years old.

    4 My nephew took his old computer **off / apart** because he wanted to see inside it.

WRITING

WRITING TIP **Opening greetings (emails)**

Use different kinds of **greetings** to write an email.

A Read the information.

Emailing someone new	Hi Chelsea, / Hello Chelsea,
	I'm Timothy, but call me Tim. I'm 14 years old.
Emailing someone you know	How are you? / How's it going? / Thanks for writing to me. / I'm writing to tell you about …

B Think about people you know. Complete the chart.

	Hobby	**How Often**	**Days of the Week**
You			
A family member			
A friend			

C Write an email. Use your notes from **B** and your own ideas to talk about hobbies.

⊠ **New message**   — ↗ ✕

To: Nina   **Subject:** Hobbies

Hi Nina,

How are you? I'm _____ . I like to _____ . I _____
a week, on _____ .

My _____ likes to _____ . (He/She) _____
a week, on _____ .
How about your family? What do they like to do on weekends?

My friend _____ likes to _____ . (He/She) _____
a week, on _____ .
What does your best friend like to do?

Write back soon!

2

WHAT DOES SHE LOOK LIKE?

PREVIEW

A Match. Join the pictures to the correct descriptions.

1 ○   ○ **a** tall   5 ○   ○ **e** mustache

2 ○   ○ **b** short   6 ○   ○ **f** beard

3 ○   ○ **c** medium height 7 ○   ○ **g** wavy

4 ○   ○ **d** braces   8 ○   ○ **h** curly

B Unscramble the words.

1 ~~u~~ b e l   _b_ _____ _u_ _____   4 l b c a k   ____ ____ ____ ____ ____

2 w r n b o   ____ ____ ____ ____ ____   5 e d r   ____ ____ ____

3 e r n e g   ____ ____ ____ ____ ____   6 d l o b n   ____ ____ ____ ____ ____

C Complete the chart. Use the words from **A**. One of the words can be used twice.

Hairstyle	Face	Body
	braces	

LANGUAGE FOCUS

A Complete the conversation.

Elena: Hi, Carrie. Look at the school magazine. There's a photo of my cousin Ben's band on page 15.

Carrie: Really? I think I have a copy here. I just found the photo. Which one is Ben? What [1] _____ he look like?

Elena: Well, [2] _____ tall and he [3] _____ blue eyes.

Carrie: Does he [4] _____ freckles?

Elena: No, that's his friend, Justin. Justin [5] _____ medium height.

Carrie: Uh-huh.

Elena: Ben [6] _____ braces.

Carrie: Oh. I found him! Cool!

B Complete the conversation. Put the sentences in the correct order.

a _____ She's tall and she has blond hair.

b _____ Is it long and curly?

c _____ Mmm … I don't know. What does she look like?

d _1_ Hi Andy, where are you? It's 4 o'clock. I'm at the baseball game.

e _____ Oh, there she is! Hey … umm … are you Andy's sister?

f _____ No, it's short and straight.

g _____ Oh, hi, Max. Sorry, I'm late. I'm still on the bus. Is my sister there?

C Look at the photo below. Complete the questions and answers.

1 _____ ? She has long hair.

2 What does Tomas look like? He has _____, curly hair.

3 _____ ? She's medium height and she has curly hair.

4 What does Daniel look like? He's tall and he wears _____.

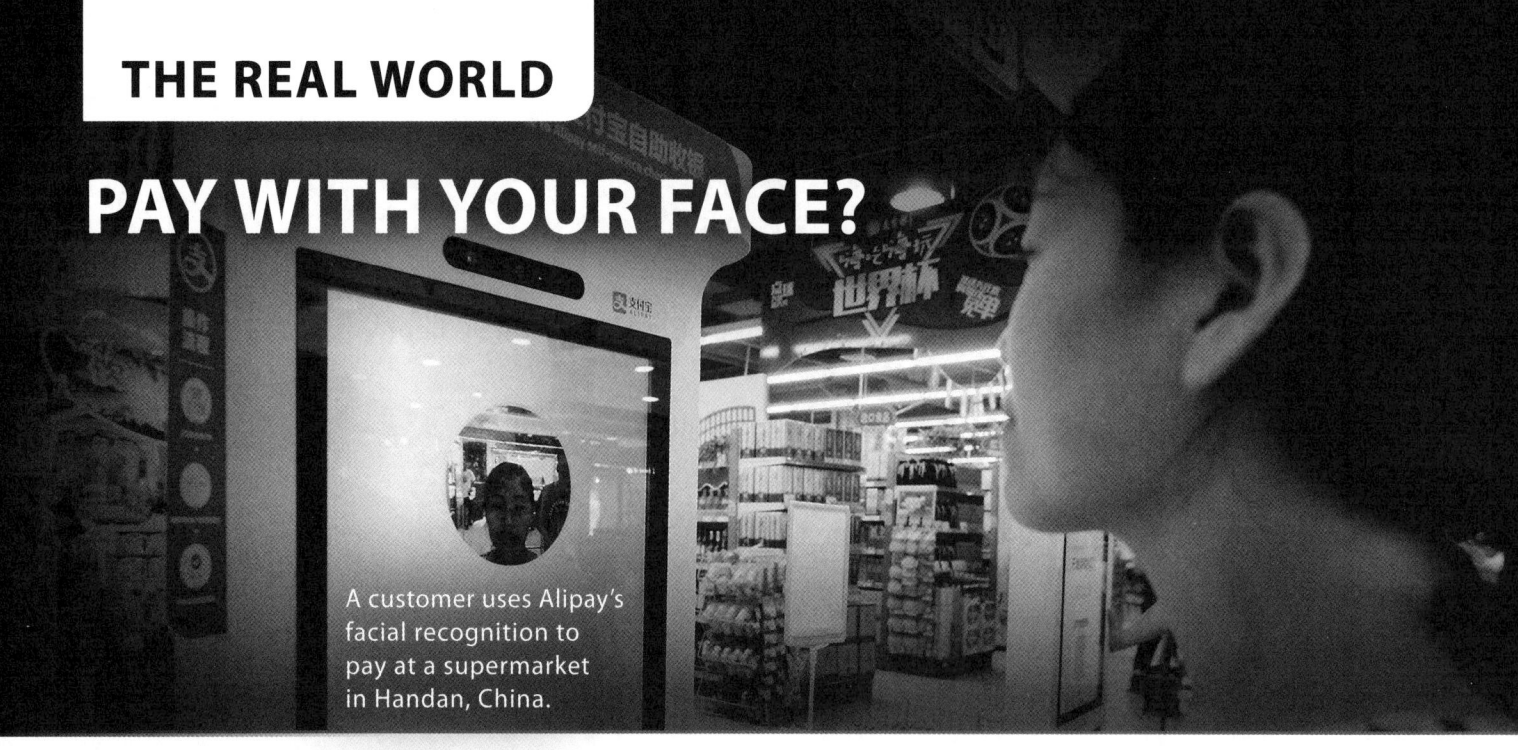

PAY WITH YOUR FACE?

A customer uses Alipay's facial recognition to pay at a supermarket in Handan, China.

How do you pay when you go shopping? Do you use cash, your phone, or your smartwatch? Technology is improving all the time, and now you can pay by facial recognition. It's easy to use.

First, you link your picture to your digital wallet. Then, you go shopping. At the store, you just stand in front of a machine. The machine recognizes who you are, so you can pay quickly. You don't even need your phone or wallet.

Lots of people love the new system. In 2019, Alipay, from China, used Dragonfly 2 in over 300 cities. WeChat's system, Frog Pro, provides a similar service for its 1.15 billion users. The number of people using facial recognition to pay for something is growing all the time.

A Read the article. Complete the summary using no more than two words from the article for each answer.

Very often, we use cash, a(n) [1] _____ , or a(n) [2] _____ to pay for things. But now, we can use [3] _____ _____ . You just connect your [4] _____ to your digital wallet, and then you can go shopping without your [5] _____ or [6] _____ . Two huge companies, [7] _____ and [8] _____ , use this technology in their payment systems, and more and more people are using it.

B Answer the questions.

1 How do you usually pay for things? _____

2 Do you want to use facial recognition to go shopping? _____

READING

A **Skim the article.** What could be another title for this article?

a Why Twins Look Alike   **b** The Lives of Twins   **c** Spot the Difference

THE SAME, BUT DIFFERENT?

Identical twins have the same physical appearance. Look at this photo of identical twins—they both have short, dark hair, and dark-colored eyes. They are the same height, and they both wear braces.

5 When you first see them, identical twins look the same, but there are some differences in their looks. Patrick Flynn, a computer scientist from the University of Notre Dame in the United States, uses computer technology to look closely at identical twins. Computers can recognize people when
10 they cut their hair or grow a beard. So how about twins? Can computers tell the difference? The answer is: Yes! While humans can tell how people feel, computers are good at noticing very small physical differences. Technology can see things like differences in the size of freckles.

So what can humans do to identify identical twins? Their personalities can be different.
15 One twin may be quiet, while the other twin may be talkative. They may also like different things and have different hobbies. Looking alike doesn't mean acting alike.

B **EXAM PRACTICE** **Answer the questions about *The Same, but Different?***

1 MAIN IDEA Identical twins are twins that _____ .

   a look very different   **b** look almost the same   **c** humans can't tell apart

2 PURPOSE The purpose of the first paragraph is _____ .

   a to give an example of how identical twins look alike

   b to show some differences between identical twins

   c to describe the boys in the photo

3 DETAIL Patrick uses technology to see differences between identical twins, such as _____ .

   a freckles   **b** hairstyles   **c** eye color

4 VOCABULARY Words like *quiet* and *talkative* may describe someone's _____ .

   a personality   **b** hobbies   **c** physical appearance

5 INFERENCE According to the article, computers probably DON'T recognize differences in _____ .

   a the shapes of eyes   **b** kinds of braces   **c** hobbies

C Answer the questions.

1 Which two words in the article have the same meaning as *the same*?

_____

2 Read the sentences below. Is each sentence a fact or an opinion? Write **F** for fact or **O** for opinion.

  a It's easy to tell identical twins apart.   _____

  b Patrick Flynn is a computer scientist.   _____

  c Identical twins can have different hobbies.   _____

VOCABULARY

A Complete the sentences. Use the words in the box.

> don't mind   alone   lifelike   creates   touch   staff

1 He _____ beautiful paintings and sells them online.

2 The food at that restaurant is delicious. I _____ waiting for a table.

3 Don't _____ that! It's very hot.

4 There are rules for the _____ . For example, everyone should keep their nails short.

5 Some video games are so _____ that they're scary!

6 I don't like to go to the movies _____—it's more fun with friends!

Leonardo da Vinci painted the *Mona Lisa* in the early 1500s.

B Complete the sentences. Circle the correct answers.

1 Some people say insects **taste** / **sound** like mushrooms.

2 On the phone, you **look** / **sound** like your mom!

3 It **feels** / **tastes** like winter, but it's still fall.

4 She **smells** / **looks** like a famous movie star.

5 What is that? It **feels** / **smells** like old eggs!

WRITING

WRITING TIP **Review: Punctuation and Capitalization**

All sentences start with a capital letter.

A   Read the information.

Most sentences end with a period (**.**). Use commas (**,**) to separate words in lists.

Questions end with a question mark (**?**). Sentences with exciting or surprising things end in an exclamation point (**!**).

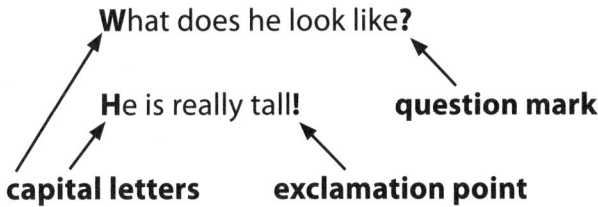

B   Write sentences. What do you look like? What about a family member and a friend?

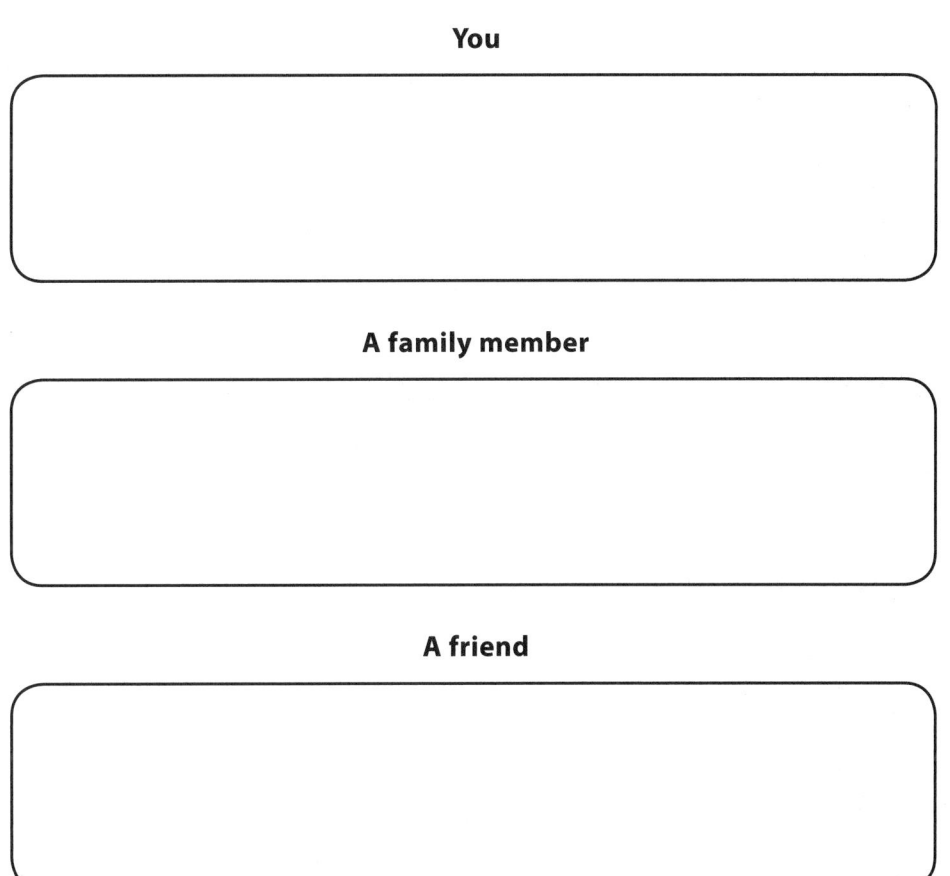

You

A family member

A friend

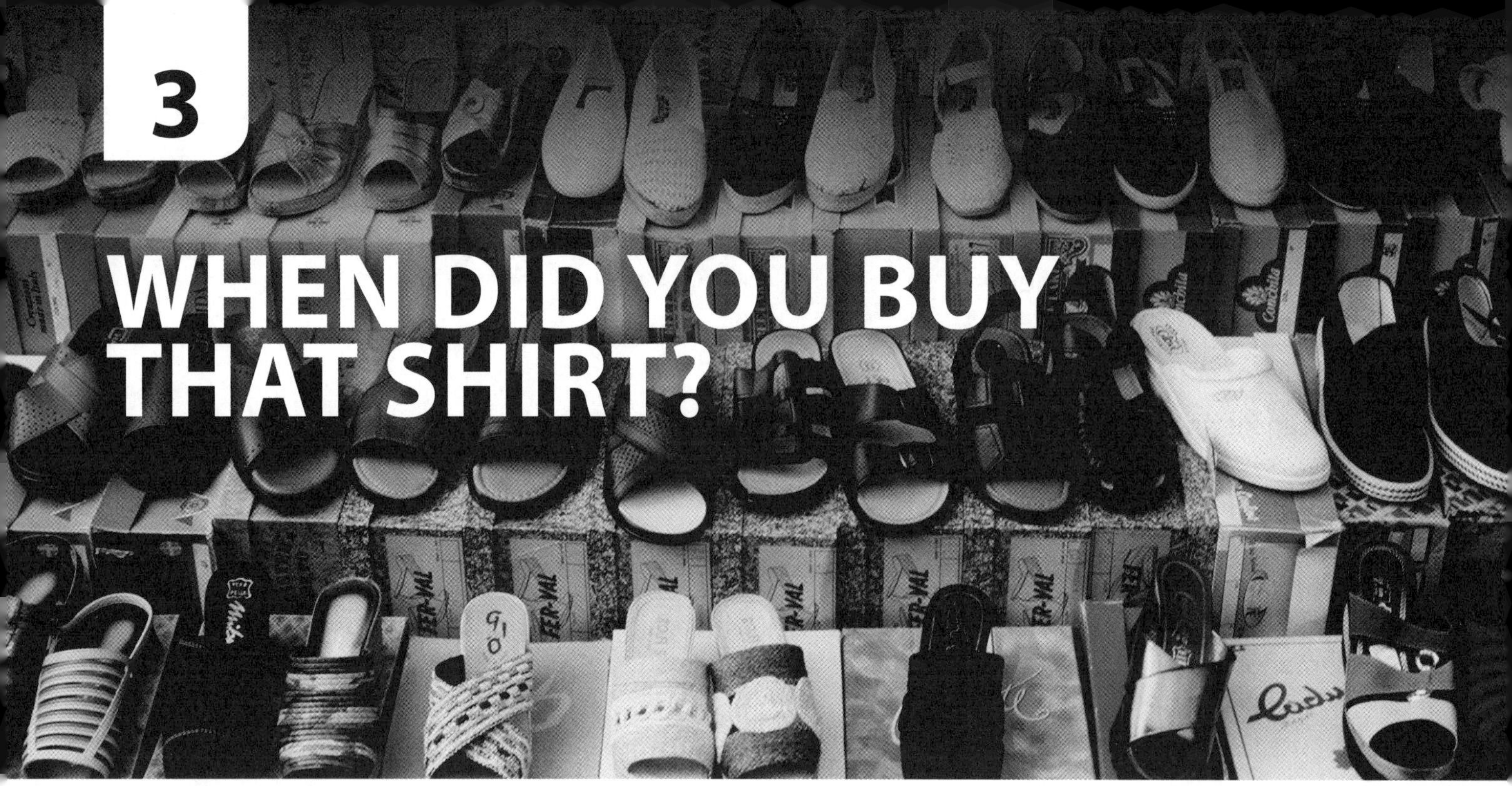

3

WHEN DID YOU BUY THAT SHIRT?

PREVIEW

A Complete the crossword puzzle. Use the pictures to help you.

Across

4 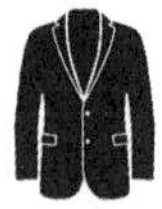

6 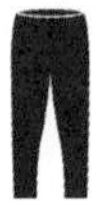

7 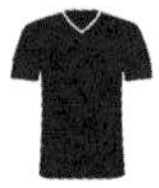

8 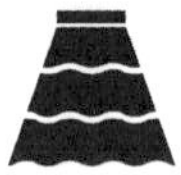

Down

1

2

3

5 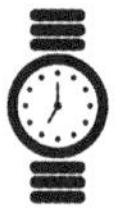

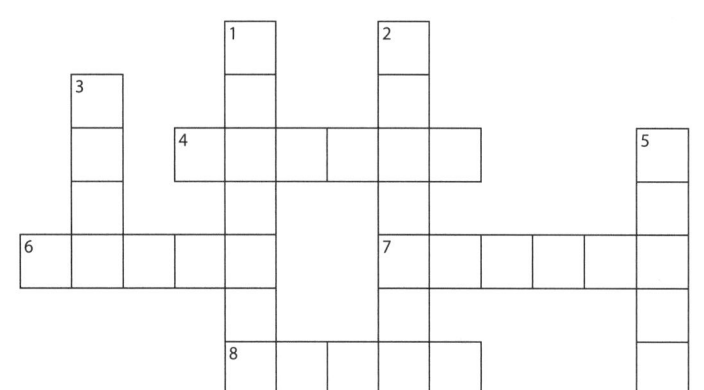

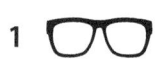

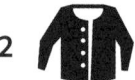

B Circle the correct answers. Which word is different?

1 jeans	pants	skirt	hat
2 sweater	wallet	T-shirt	jacket
3 glasses	dress	jeans	shirt
4 wallet	pants	watch	backpack

C Write. Which items in **A** and **B** do you usually wear every day?

____

____

LANGUAGE FOCUS

A Complete the conversation. Use the words in the box.

couple did last ago recently just

Donna: Hi, Linda, I love your jacket! Did you get it [1]_____?

Linda: Thanks, Donna. Yeah, I [2]_____ got it last weekend.

Donna: Cool! I want to get a new jacket, too.

Linda: Why? Your jacket is really nice. When [3]_____ you buy it?

Donna: Well, I bought it a(n) [4]_____ of years [5]_____.

Linda: Really? I think it's great, and it goes well with your purple shoes, too.

Donna: Thanks. I bought them three days ago—I mean, [6]_____ Friday.

B Complete the conversation. Put the words in the correct order to make sentences.

Mom: Michelle, are you ready?

Michelle: No! / soccer / can't / I / my / find / uniform

1 _____.

Mom: ago / we / one / days / bought / just / the / two / it / Is

2 _____?

Michelle: No, / got / two years / I / the one / ago

3 _____.

Mom: in / car / think / the / it's / I

4 _____.

Michelle: Thanks, Mom. / where / my / are / And / sneakers

5 _____?

Mom: They're in the car, too.

Michelle: Great. Let's go!

C Write. Complete the questions and answers.

1 I like your shoes. [1]_____ get [2]_____ recently?

Yes, [3]_____ last night.

2 When [4]_____ your shirt?

[5]_____ two weeks ago.

3 [6]_____ new jeans?

Yes, I just [7]_____ a couple of days [8]_____.

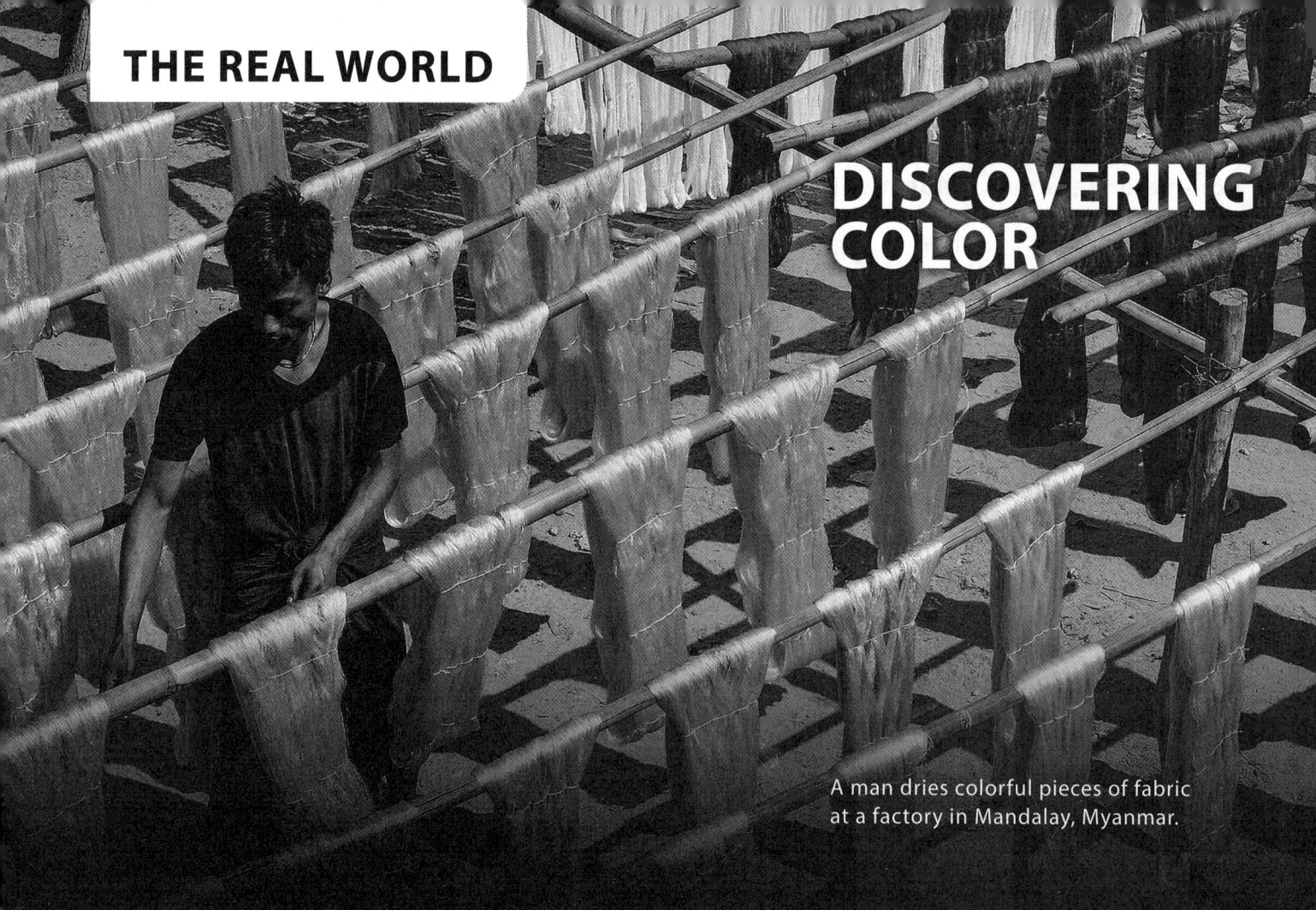

DISCOVERING COLOR

A man dries colorful pieces of fabric at a factory in Mandalay, Myanmar.

A Skim the article. What is it about?

  a what colors mean   **b** the history of dyes   **c** why colors are important

Can you imagine a world without colors? We could still eat, sleep, and work, but life would be boring.

Colored clothes go back to 2,600 B.C. People made colors—called dyes—with plants, parts of animals, and other natural substances. They mixed these things with water and oil and used them to dye clothes and jewelry. In many parts of the world, people used yellow dyes because they could get them from different plants. Some colors were rare. For example, indigo—a kind of blue dye—came from plants that were specific to India and Southeast Asia.

The shellfish necessary to make purple was only found on one side of the Mediterranean Sea. It took thousands of them to make purple cloth. Because of this, purple was the rarest color, used for kings and queens. Purple clothes gave people power and status.

B Complete the sentences about *Discovering Color*. Circle the correct answers.

People started to ¹ **make / dye** clothes around 4,600 years ago. They used ² **parts of trees / plastic** to make some dyes. Yellow was ³ **more / less** common than blue. Purple was probably the most expensive dye because people used ⁴ **a lot of shellfish / rare plants** to make it.

READING

A Skim the article. What could be another title for this article?

a Recycling Glass Bottles

b Waste Paper Problems

c Using Trash in New Ways

WEARABLE TRASH

Lots of things can be recycled—glass, paper, metal, and plastic. Rethink Fabrics is a company based in Las Vegas, the United States. It's trying to fight the planet's plastic waste problem, one bottle at a time.

5 The company's goal is to encourage people to think about where their clothes come from by making clothing from trash. It uses new technology to make clothing like T-shirts.

Rethink Fabrics' T-shirts are high quality and not very expensive. They are made from recycled plastic bottles.
10 Each T-shirt shows the number of plastic bottles used to make it, so customers know they are helping the planet.

At the end of the T-shirt's life, the recycling process continues. The company can make an old T-shirt into another new piece of clothing. Other companies recycle
15 plastic waste into shoes, and even outdoor items like park benches. Look around and discover new ways to recycle. Your plastic really can help to save the environment!

B EXAM PRACTICE **Complete the summary.** Use the words in the box.

expensive   T-shirts   plastic bottles   recycles   help   environment

Do you think about how you can save the ¹ _____? Rethink Fabrics is trying to
² _____ the planet. The company makes ³ _____ from
⁴ _____. The clothes are high quality but not ⁵ _____.
When the T-shirts are old, Rethink Fabrics ⁶ _____ them to make T-shirts again.

C Answer the questions.

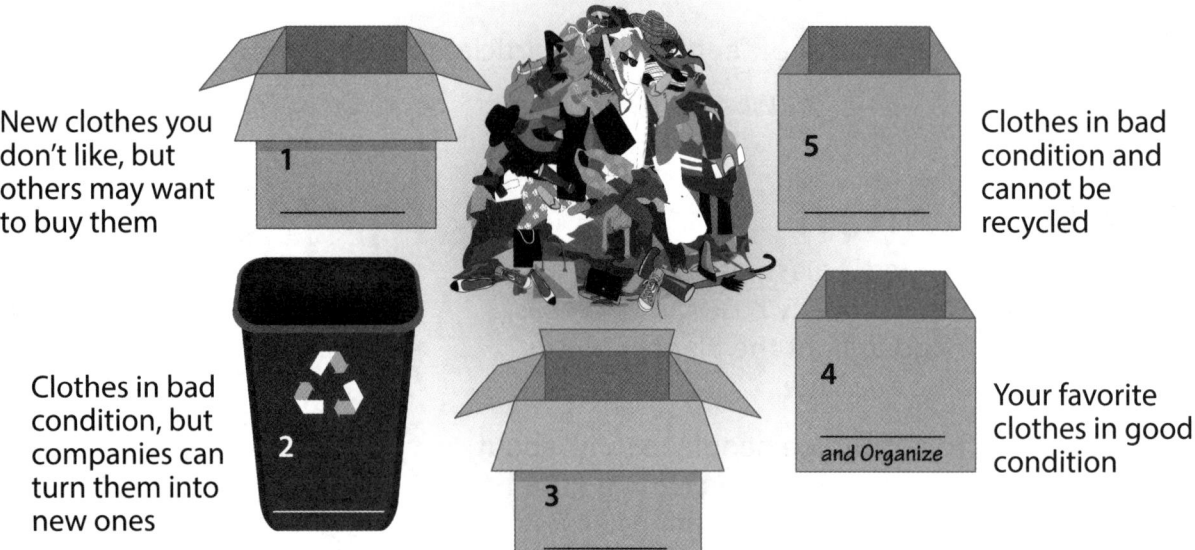

WHAT TO DO WITH OLD CLOTHES

New clothes you don't like, but others may want to buy them — 1 _____

Clothes in bad condition, but companies can turn them into new ones — 2 _____

Clothes you don't like, but are in good condition — 3 _____

5 _____ Clothes in bad condition and cannot be recycled

4 _____ and Organize — Your favorite clothes in good condition

1 Complete the diagram above. Use the words in the box.

> Trash   Donate   Sell   Recycle   Keep

2 What do you do with your old clothes?

_____

VOCABULARY

A Complete the sentences. Use the words in the box.

> environment   in a row   rural   whole   discovered   wrapped

1 She _____ a scarf around her neck.

2 The city is nice, but I live in a(n) _____ area and I really like it.

3 The students had tests three days _____, so all of them were tired.

4 There are over 7 billion people in the _____ world.

5 Zookeepers create a safe and clean _____ for animals to live in.

6 In 1781, astronomer William Herschel _____ the planet Uranus.

B Complete the sentences. Circle the correct answers.

1 It's so hot! Why don't you **take off** / **try on** your jacket?

2 It's raining. Don't forget to **take off** / **put on** your raincoat.

3 I want some new jeans. Can I **try on** / **put on** that pair?

WRITING

WRITING TIP **Using** *because*

Use *because* to join two short sentences. The sentence after *because* has the reason for the idea in the other sentence.

A Read the information.

They make T-shirts from plastic bottles. They want to save the environment.

They make T-shirts from plastic bottles **because** they want to save the environment.

B Read the comments in the forum below. Write a reply about your favorite outfit.

Discussion

What's your favorite outfit and why?

Comments

Max	**August 11 8:55 p.m.**

Hi. My name is Max.
I live in Oslo, Norway. I wear jeans because it's often cold here. I like to wear T-shirts and a jacket with my jeans.

Jessie	**August 11 8:59 p.m.**

My favorite outfit is an old purple and black dress. I love it because it's always in fashion. I usually wear it to parties with high heels.

Reena	**August 11 9:05 p.m.**

Hey, everyone.
I'm Reena. I play a lot of sports, so I often wear shorts, a T-shirt, and sneakers. This is my favorite outfit because it's so comfortable.

Me	**August 11 9:15 p.m.**

_____

_____

_____

4

WHAT'S THE COLDEST PLACE ON EARTH?

PREVIEW

A **Complete the puzzle.** Use the chart.

1	2	3	4	5	6	7	8	9	10	11
a	c	d	e	i	k	l	m	n	o	s

1 t r e e
       4 4

2 __ __ __ __ __ __ __
       1   4   1 7 7

3 __ __ __
   10 2 6

4 __ __ __ __ __ __
   2 10   9

5 __ __ __ __ __
   3   11

6 __ __ __ __ __ __ __ __
   8 10   9   5 9

7 __ __ __ __ __
      7 1   4

B **Write.** Which adjectives describe size? Which describe temperature? Use the words in the box.

> biggest hottest largest coldest tallest smallest highest lowest

Size: _____ _____ _____ _____

Temperature: _____ _____ _____ _____

C **Write.** Make two quiz questions about places in your country. Use some of the words in **B**.

1 What's the largest desert in Peru? _____

2 _____

3 _____

LANGUAGE FOCUS

A Match. Join the two parts of the conversation.

1 Hi, Lee. What are you doing? ○   ○ **a** Ummm, Antarctica?

2 I love geography! I can help you. ○   ○ **b** The Amazon rainforest?

3 Sure! How long is the Nile River? ○   ○ **c** I think it's about 6,650 kilometers.

4 Correct. What's the coldest continent in the world? ○   ○ **d** Great, thanks! Ask me a question then, please.

5 That's right! What's the largest rainforest in the world? ○   ○ **e** Hey! That's not a geography question!

6 Uh-huh. Last question. Where's the most popular café near here? ○   ○ **f** Oh, hi, Lisa. I'm studying for my geography exam.

7 I know, but I'm really thirsty. Let's go get a drink!

B Correct one mistake in each question.

1 What's hottest place near you?

2 What's the goodest food in your country?

3 What's the most popularest mountain on your continent?

4 What's the most biggest store near your house?

5 Where's the place most beautiful in your country?

6 What's the famousest city in your country?

C Write sentences and questions using the words. Use the superlative form of the adjectives.

1 Who / tall / person / world

_____?

2 place / cold / What / world

_____?

3 Africa / high / mountain / Mount Kilimanjaro

_____.

4 country / world / large / What

_____?

5 small / world / continent / Australia

_____.

Mount Kilimanjaro,
Tanzania

THE REAL WORLD

REINDEER IN THE WILD

Reindeer in Lapland, Finland

A Complete the article. Use the words in the box.

> grow   coldest   plants   warm   long

Reindeer live in some of the ¹ _____ places in Europe, Asia, and North America. In North America, reindeer are called caribou.

Reindeer are herbivores, meaning they eat only ² _____ . They live in groups called herds. Herds of reindeer often travel over ³ _____ distances—walking as much as 5,000 kilometers every year. Male reindeer lose their antlers and then ⁴ _____ new ones every year. Their antlers grow up to 140 centimeters in length!

Reindeer live in cold places, so how do they stay warm? One way is that their noses warm the cold air before it travels into their bodies. Their bodies also have lots of fur—all the way from their noses to their feet! The fur keeps their bodies ⁵ _____ against the wind and the cold.

B Complete the sentences. Use words from the article.

> It grows new ¹ _____ every year.

> Its ² _____ makes cold air warm.

> ³ _____ on its body protects it from the cold.

READING

A Look at the photo. What do you think the article is about?

a plants in the desert   **b** what a desert is   **c** desert tourism

FULL OF LIFE

When you hear the word "desert," what
words do you think of? Many people
think of the word "hot." The hottest
weather ever recorded on our planet,
5 57°C, was in a desert called Death Valley,
in the United States. But not all deserts
are hot. There are also cold deserts.
Antarctica has the largest desert in the
world, and it's very cold there.

10 Some people think nothing lives in
deserts. But this isn't true. More than
one billion people live in the world's
deserts. There are also insects, birds, and
other animal species that live there—like
15 snakes and lizards.

Camels are an important form of transportation in deserts.

So what makes an area a desert? Well, scientists agree that all deserts are dry. A real desert
gets no more than 25 centimeters of rain or snow a year. This means people, animals, and
plants have very little water to drink. They have to learn to live in these extreme places.

B   EXAM PRACTICE   **Read the article.** Circle **T** for True, **F** for False, or **NG** for Not Given.

1	Death Valley is the driest place in the United States.	**T**	**F**	**NG**
2	Fewer than one million people live in deserts.	**T**	**F**	**NG**
3	Most desert animals are active at night.	**T**	**F**	**NG**
4	The desert in Antarctica gets more than 25 centimeters of rain or snow a year.	**T**	**F**	**NG**
5	The animals in deserts live with only a little water.	**T**	**F**	**NG**

C Write. Correct the false sentence(s) in **B**.

_____

_____

_____

_____

VOCABULARY

A Complete the sentences. Use the words in the box.

> insect   species   flow   planet   gentle   lose

1 Every year we _____ some languages. This is called language death.

2 Earth is the third _____ from the sun.

3 I love giraffes because they look so _____ .

4 Scientists discover new _____ of plants and animals all the time.

5 Beetles are a kind of _____ .

6 Rivers _____ into oceans, but sometimes it is a long trip!

B Write. Write the numbers or words.

1 zero point two _____

2 half _____

3 2,000,000 _____

4 nine thousand seven hundred _____

5 80,000 _____

The Louvre, the largest museum in the world, covers an area of 72,735 square meters.

WRITING

WRITING TIP **Using commas**

Use commas to give more information.

A Read the information.

Use two commas in the middle of a sentence to give more information.

The hottest weather ever recorded on our planet, 57°C, was in a desert called Death Valley, in the United States.

comma　　**comma**

Use one comma at the end of the sentence to give more information.

The hottest weather ever recorded was in Death Valley, a desert.

comma

B Complete the chart. Describe an extreme place.

Name of an extreme place	
Where is it?	
In what way(s) is it extreme?	
Give example(s) to show why it is extreme.	

C Write a short paragraph about an extreme place. Use the information in B.

_____

_____

_____

_____

_____

ARE PARROTS SMARTER THAN PEOPLE?

PREVIEW

A Label the pictures. Use the words in the box.

> monkey   turtle   rabbit   rhino   horse   parrot   dog

1 _____

2 _____

3 _____

4 _____

5 _____

6 _____

7 _____

B Circle the correct answers. Which animals do the adjectives describe best?

1 tiny   **rats / dolphins**

2 dangerous   **rabbits / snakes**

3 heavy   **penguins / whales**

4 fast   **turtles / horses**

C Write. Which do you think are scarier, lions or sharks? Why?

_____

_____

LANGUAGE FOCUS

A Complete the conversations. Circle the correct answers.

1 Tom: Which are [1] **playfuller / more playful**, horses or rabbits?

Brian: Hmm … I guess rabbits are, but I like horses [2] **more better / better**.

Tom: Really? Why?

Brian: Well, horses are [3] **more intelligent / intelligenter** and [4] **friendlier / friendlyer**.

2 Sara: I want to get a pet snake. I think they're [5] **more cute / cuter** than dogs!

Beth: Really? I think snakes are [6] **scary / more scary**.

Sara: Not all snakes. I don't want a [7] **dangerous / more dangerous** one.

B Look at the chart. Complete the questions and answers.

		Height	Population in Antarctica	Weight	Swimming Speed
Emperor penguin		About 115 cm	600,000	Up to 40 kg	Up to 12 kph
	Adélie penguin	About 70 cm	More than six million	4 to 5.5 kg	Up to 8 kph

1 Which penguin is taller? _____ .

2 Which penguin has a larger population in Antarctica? _____ .

3 _____? The emperor penguin is heavier.

4 _____? The Adélie penguin is slower.

C Complete the conversation. Put the words in the correct order to make sentences.

Hayley: Hi, Tom. Do you want to watch a TV show about animals in the sea?

Tom: do / OK, cool! / like / sea animals / Which / you

1 _____?

Hayley: sharks / because / more interesting / I like / than dolphins / they're

2 _____ .

Tom: more intelligent / Yes, but / dolphins are / than sharks

3 _____ .

Hayley: dolphins / Which are / or sharks / That's true! / faster,

4 _____?

Tom: Let's watch the show and find out!

TALKING MONKEYS

A putty-nosed monkey

A Predict. How do monkeys communicate with each other?

Putty-nosed monkeys live in rainforests in Africa. Scientists are studying how these monkeys make noises to communicate with each other. For example, scientists believe they make the sounds *hack* and *pyow* to communicate danger. The monkeys use *hack* to warn others about a leopard, and they shout *pyow* when they spot an eagle.

Scientists believe the monkeys can put sounds together into "sentences." They start with *pyow* and end with *hack*. The monkeys also change the number of times they make each sound in a sentence to mean different things. For example, a sentence of three *pyows* followed by up to four *hacks* seems to mean "Let's go!" Scientists believe there's still a lot that we can learn about putty-nosed monkeys' communication.

B Read the article. Circle **T** for True, **F** for False, or **NG** for Not Given.

1	Putty-nosed monkeys live in groups of up to 30 monkeys.	T	F	NG
2	Putty-nosed monkeys use *hack* when they are happy.	T	F	NG
3	Putty-nosed monkeys probably think that eagles are dangerous.	T	F	NG
4	Scientists study the lengths of *pyow-hack* sentences to predict how far putty-nosed monkeys travel.	T	F	NG

READING

A Skim the article. The article does NOT talk about how emperor penguins _____ .

a keep warm   **b** hunt for food   **c** look after their young

SURVIVING THE WINTER

Emperor penguins are really intelligent. This is why they can stay in Antarctica all year round. It's colder than any of the other continents—as low as –60ºC. This makes it too cold for many animals to stay there during
5 the winter months, but emperor penguins do it.

In winter, they spend long periods of time standing in a big circle. This protects them from the cold and the wind. The emperor penguins work as a team. They take turns standing on the inside of the circle (where it's
10 warmer), and then on the outside. They never get too cold, even in extreme weather conditions.

Emperor penguins are intelligent in another way. The mother lays her egg around June. Then she leaves it behind, and goes to the ocean to look for food. The father keeps the egg on his feet for
15 about two months. During that time, the egg cannot touch the cold, icy ground. The mother comes back and feeds the new baby penguin. Only emperor penguins lay their eggs in the middle of winter, showing how special and amazing they are.

An emperor penguin colony in Atka Bay, Antarctica

B `EXAM PRACTICE` **Answer the questions about *Surviving the Winter*.**

1 `REFERENCE` In line 5, *do it* means to stay in Antarctica _____ .

   a for a month   **b** during the winter   **c** during the summer

2 `DETAIL` The outside of the circle is _____ the inside.

   a warmer than   **b** colder than   **c** the same temperature as

3 `VOCABULARY` The phrase *extreme weather conditions* in line 11 means _____ .

   a comfortable temperatures   **b** hot, then cold temperatures   **c** really cold temperatures

4 `INFERENCE` For two months, the father penguin probably _____ .

   a looks for food   **b** stays with the mother   **c** doesn't eat

5 `DETAIL` In Antarctica, it is _____ in June.

   a winter   **b** fall   **c** summer

C **Match the sentences to the animals.** Write the letters (**a–e**) next to the correct names.

a It keeps its egg on its feet.

b It uses sounds to form "sentences."

c It works with other animals to keep warm.

d It lives in a rainforest.

e It lives in Antarctica.

1	Putty-nosed monkey	
2	Emperor penguin	

VOCABULARY

A **Complete the sentences.** Use the words in the box.

> pets   job   sick   well   spend   in trouble

1 How do you usually _____ your weekend?

2 I want a(n) _____ that's interesting, maybe as a scientist.

3 I didn't do my homework, so I got _____ with my teacher.

4 Many people keep dogs and cats as _____ .

5 You're _____ —get some rest and get _____ soon.

B **Write.** Use the words in the box to write sentences with the same meaning.

> sick   search   rescued   faster   incredible

1 Horses are quicker than people.

_____

2 Our teacher was ill, so we had a different teacher yesterday.

_____

3 They saved the child from the fire.

_____

4 Use the internet to look for the answer.

_____

5 The mimic octopus is an amazing animal—it can change its body shape to look like other animals.

_____

_____

WRITING

WRITING TIP **Giving more information**

Use **parentheses ( )** to give more information. We can take the information out of the sentence and still understand it.

A Read the information.

They take turns standing on the inside of the circle **(**where it's warmer**)**, and then on the outside.

explains why they stand on the inside of the circle

They take turns standing on the inside of the circle, and then on the outside.

without the information the sentence is still clear

B Complete the chart. Write about an animal you want to see and why. Use your ideas.

Animal you want to see	
Description of the Animal	
Information About the Animal	

C Write a short report. Describe an animal you want to see. Use your notes from **B**. Use parentheses to give more information.

_____

_____

_____

_____

_____

6

I REALLY LIKE ELECTRONIC MUSIC!

PREVIEW

A Complete the puzzle. Use the letters in the picture.

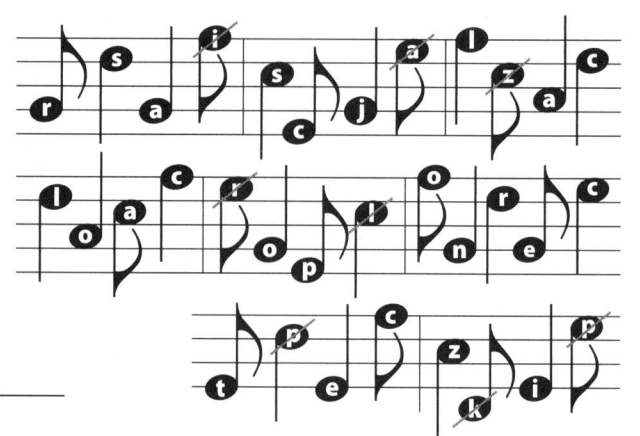

1 __r__ __a__ __p__
2 ___ ___ ___ ___ ___ ___ ___ ___ __l__
3 ___ ___ __z__ ___
4 ___ ___ ___ __k__
5 __p__ ___ ___
6 ___ ___ ___ ___ ___ ___ __i__ ___

B Circle the correct answers. Which word is different?

1 rock   guitar   pop   rap

2 awesome   cool   electronic   great

3 album   classical   jazz   electronic

4 group   singer   band   pop

C Write. Answer the questions.

1 What kind of music do people in your family usually listen to? _____

2 Which do you like better, classical or pop music? _____

LANGUAGE FOCUS

A **Correct one mistake in each question.**

1 What kind of music you like best?

2 Which you like better, pop or rock?

3 What do you like better, Ariana Grande or Thomas Rhett?

4 Do you classical music?

5 Which do you better like, electronic music or pop music?

B **Complete the interview.** Circle the correct answers.

Interviewer: I'm at a music festival talking to students. So, Victoria, ¹ **what** / **who** kind of music do you like best?

Victoria: I like rock music the ² **better** / **best**.

Interviewer: Cool! Do you like the Mysterines?

Victoria: I love ³ **them** / **it**!

Interviewer: And ⁴ **which** / **who** do you like better, Beyoncé or Lady Gaga?

Victoria: I like Lady Gaga ⁵ **best** / **better** than Beyoncé.

C **Complete the sentences.** Use the words in the box.

like	don't like	love	can't stand	OK

1 ★☆☆☆ I _____ loud music.

2 ★★★☆ I _____ rock music.

3 ★★★★ I _____ to listen to music.

4 ☆☆☆☆ I _____ classical music.

5 ★★☆☆ I think rap music is _____ .

A music festival in London, England

THE WEIGHTLESS SONG

A Scan the article. Marconi Union is a(n) _____ band.

a British   b Canadian   c American

Marconi Union is a band from England. They made a piece of music named "Weightless," which scientists believe is more relaxing than any other song. The music has sounds of instruments, such as the piano and the guitar, natural sounds, and singing voices.

The music is eight minutes long. It starts fast and then slows down. The rhythm is very important because our heartbeat matches it, and gradually slows down with the music.

As we listen, our brain relaxes. The music slows the heart rate and reduces stress.

Scientists say the music is more relaxing than a cup of tea, a walk, or even a massage. It's the perfect song for resting at the end of a long day!

B Read the article. Circle **T** for True or **F** for False.

1 Scientists made the song "Weightless."	T	F
2 There are sounds of nature in the song.	T	F
3 The beginning of the song is slower than the end.	T	F
4 The song can change the speed of our heartbeat.	T	F

READING

A **Scan the article.** Which of the following is NOT mentioned in the article?

a Beethoven was a teacher.

b Beethoven played the viola.

c Beethoven moved to Vienna when he was 22 years old.

MAKING MUSIC

Ludwig van Beethoven is a well-known musician, born in 1770 in Germany. But did you know he was deaf? During his life, he wrote many different pieces of music for orchestras. He also played several
5 instruments, including the piano and the viola.

Beethoven taught many students, but he also had some famous teachers—like Haydn and Neefe. They all saw his amazing musical abilities. When he lived in Vienna, Austria, he often performed for very
10 important people.

Unfortunately, he lost his hearing completely by the age of 40. At that time, people didn't understand deafness. Beethoven's friends wrote questions in notebooks, and Beethoven continued to speak to
15 them. He didn't quit writing music, and he got a lot of his musical ideas while taking walks. Amazingly, he is most famous for some of the pieces of music he wrote after he lost his hearing! Today, many people around the world continue to play his music.

A portrait of Ludwig van Beethoven painted by Joseph Karl Stieler in 1819

B **EXAM PRACTICE** **Answer the questions about *Making Music.***

1 DETAIL Beethoven was born in _____ .

  a Germany   b Austria   c Italy

2 VOCABULARY Another way of saying *he was deaf* is *he could not* _____ .

  a see   b smell   c hear

3 INFERENCE Beethoven is famous for his _____ music.

  a pop   b classical   c rock

4 REFERENCE In line 12, the phrase *at that time* refers to _____ .

  a 1770   b 1810   c 1840

5 DETAIL To help him create music pieces, Beethoven _____ .

  a wrote to his friends   b chatted with friends   c took walks

C Answer the questions.

1 Label the pictures. Use the words in the box.

> guitar   cello   piano   trumpet   drum   harp

1 _____   4 _____

2 _____   5 _____

3 _____   6 _____

2 What kind of music do you like best? What are some common musical instruments used to

create this kind of music? _____

VOCABULARY

A Complete the sentences. Use the words in the box.

> concerts   floor   well-known   perform   decide   instrument

1 My favorite musical _____ is the guitar.

2 Albert Einstein was a(n) _____ scientist.

3 She slipped and fell on the wet _____.

4 I love to watch ballet dancers _____ *The Nutcracker.*

5 My favorite band played 75 _____ last year.

6 I can't _____ what I want to study in college because there are
so many choices.

B Match. Join the two parts of the sentences.

1 A large crowd of soccer fans   ○   ○ **a** was quiet throughout the performance.

2 About half of the class   ○   ○ **b** performed at this concert hall yesterday.

3 The concert audience   ○   ○ **c** waited to go into the stadium.

4 My favorite band   ○   ○ **d** has nine players on the field.

5 A baseball team   ○   ○ **e** were late for the test.

WRITING

WRITING TIP **Expressing personal opinions**

Use positive and negative language to express your **personal opinions**.

A Read the review.

Positive opinions

> I really like …
> I love …

Negative opinions

> I don't like …
> I can't stand …

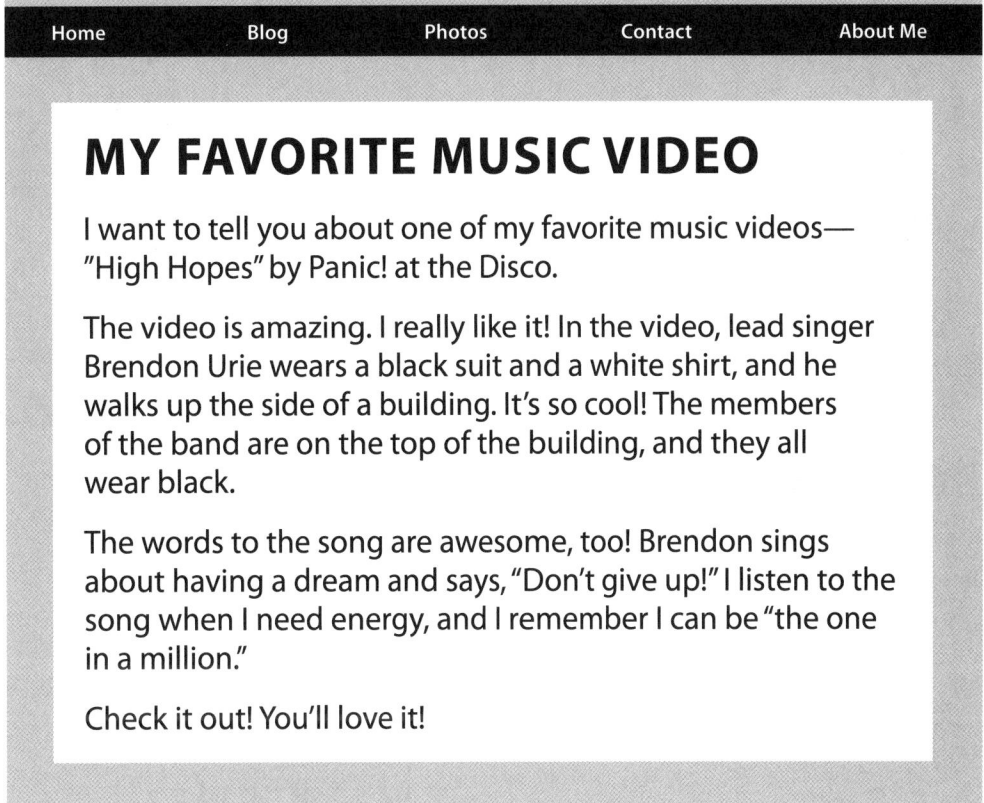

| Home | Blog | Photos | Contact | About Me |

MY FAVORITE MUSIC VIDEO

I want to tell you about one of my favorite music videos—"High Hopes" by Panic! at the Disco.

The video is amazing. I really like it! In the video, lead singer Brendon Urie wears a black suit and a white shirt, and he walks up the side of a building. It's so cool! The members of the band are on the top of the building, and they all wear black.

The words to the song are awesome, too! Brendon sings about having a dream and says, "Don't give up!" I listen to the song when I need energy, and I remember I can be "the one in a million."

Check it out! You'll love it!

B Think about a music video you know. Complete the chart. Use your own ideas.

Title of Music Video	
Description of the Music Video	
Positive or Negative Opinions of the Music Video	

C Write a music video review. Use your notes from **B**.

WHAT'S FOR DINNER?

PREVIEW

A Complete the crossword puzzle. Use the pictures to help you.

Across

4

5

Down

1

2

3

6

B Look at the items in A. Circle those that you can cut.

C Complete the chart. Use the words in the box.

fork glass plate knife cup bowl spoon

Things to Eat With	Things You Eat From	Things to Put Drinks In
fork		

LANGUAGE FOCUS

A Complete the conversations. Use *there is, there are,* and other words.

1 **Maria:** [1] _____ milk in the refrigerator?

   Ben: No, [2] _____ .

2 **Diego:** [3] _____ napkins in the cabinet?

   Sofia: No, [4] _____ , but there [5] _____ some on the counter.

3 **Jenny:** [6] _____ plates in the sink?

   Sam: Yes, [7] _____ .

4 **Jack:** Let's have something sweet. [8] _____ ice cream?

   Ying: Yes, [9] _____ .

5 **Ana:** There [10] _____ any forks on the table. Where are they?

   Luka: They're on the counter. There [11] _____ some next to the sink, too.

B Complete the conversation. Put the sentences in the correct order.

a _____ Hey, Marco! Sure. When is it?

b _____ Oh, that's in three days! What do you need?

c _____ Thanks! Sandra and I bought some cupcakes and juice as well.

d __1__ Hi, David! Can you help me get ready for Izzy's surprise birthday party?

e _____ No, there aren't. But I can buy some.

f _____ We need some bowls and spoons. Are there any left from the festival?

g _____ Great! It's on Saturday.

h _____ Awesome! I can't wait! See you on Saturday.

C Complete the conversation. Circle the correct answers.

Katy: Let's make [1] **any / some** sandwiches for lunch.

Jeff: Sure. [2] **There's / There are** some bread on the counter.

Katy: That's great. What do we have in the refrigerator?

Jeff: Let me see. There are [3] **any / some** tomatoes and [4] **there's / there are** some meat. [5] **There's / There are** also some cheese.

Katy: Hmm … Is there [6] **any / some** juice?

Jeff: No, there [7] **isn't / aren't**. But I can buy some from the supermarket.

Katy: OK. Can you buy some onions, too? There [8] **isn't / aren't** any in the kitchen.

DARK DINING

Guests having a meal at Dans Le Noir
in London, England

A Scan the article. When did dark dining start? _____

B Complete the article. Use the words in the box.

> popular   taste   see   senses   sight   table

Restaurants usually spend a lot of time making food look—not just taste—good. But what about a

restaurant where you [1] _____ your food, but can't see it?

Dark dining is a different way to eat food. It happens in a dark restaurant where you can't

[2] _____ the food you eat. You don't know exactly what you're eating. You guess the

dishes, and after the meal, your waiter describes the food.

One restaurant, Dans Le Noir, describes how dark dining is different. The main idea is that when you

can't see the food, your other four [3] _____—taste, smell, touch, and hearing—increase.

This can make the food seem even more delicious. In Dans Le Noir, you sit at a long

[4] _____, but can't see who is sitting next to you. This means getting to know people

in an unusual way—in the dark. Many dark dining restaurants also support people with

[5] _____ problems—people who are blind often work in these restaurants.

The first dark dining restaurant opened in 1999 in Zurich, Switzerland. Now, dark dining is

[6] _____ around the world. Today, many places—such as London, New York, Barcelona,

Seoul, and Singapore—have these restaurants.

READING

A **Scan the article.** How much poutine did Joey Chestnut eat? _____

FRIES LIKE NO OTHERS

Poutine is a popular dish in Canada—you can find it everywhere from fast-food chains to fine dining restaurants. It started in Warwick, Quebec, in 1957, but it's now popular around the world. In the beginning,
5 poutine was made of French fries, cheese curds, and meat sauce. Today, people add various toppings, such as mushrooms, to create different types of poutine.

There are poutine eating contests around the world. Smoke's Poutinerie World Poutine Eating
10 Championship is one of the most famous. Every year, people go to Toronto and try to eat the most poutine in 10 minutes. The first place prize is $6,000. The competition also collects money to help children go to summer camps.

15 Joey Chestnut, an American competitive eater, set the world record on October 19, 2019. He ate over 12.7 kilograms of poutine in just 10 minutes.

Joey Chestnut won the 2018 World Poutine Eating Championship in Toronto, Canada.

B **EXAM PRACTICE** **Read the article.** Circle **T** for True, **F** for False, or **NG** for Not Given.

1 People began to eat poutine more than 100 years ago.	**T** **F** **NG**	
2 Traditionally, chefs make poutine with three kinds of food.	**T** **F** **NG**	
3 Smoke's Poutinerie World Poutine Eating Championship is the largest in the world.	**T** **F** **NG**	
4 Children learn about poutine at the summer camps.	**T** **F** **NG**	
5 Before 2019, no one ate more than 12.7 kilograms of poutine in a competition.	**T** **F** **NG**	

There are more than 50 varieties of poutine.

C **Complete the sentences.** Use the words in the box.

> cook   cut   pour   mix

HOW TO MAKE POUTINE

1 _____ potatoes into fries.

2 _____ the fries in a pan.

3 Place the fries in a bowl and _____ them with cheese curds.

4 _____ gravy over the fries and cheese curds.

VOCABULARY

A **Complete the sentences.** Use the words in the box.

> comes from   thin   various   delicious   hungry   chef

1 Students in this class learn _____ ways to fold napkins.

2 Look at all of those cookies and cupcakes! They all look _____ .

3 That restaurant is always busy because the _____ studied at a famous cooking school.

4 She cuts the tomato into _____ slices.

5 It's almost lunch time, but I'm not really _____ .

6 Which fruit _____ trees?

B **Write.** Describe the food. Use the words in the box.

> salty   bitter   sour   sweet

1

_____

3

_____

2

_____

4

_____

WRITING

WRITING TIP **Using informal and semi-formal writing**

Use informal and semi-formal writing for different things.

A Read the information.

Informal

For writing blog posts, text messages, emails, and letters to friends and close family.

> Hey Vera!
>
> How are you doing?
>
> See ya!

Semi-formal

For writing school reports, homework, letters, and emails to people you don't know well.

> Dear Vera,
>
> I hope you're well.
>
> I look forward to hearing from you.

B Read the email from Vera. Make notes about a popular food in your country. Use the questions in the email to help you.

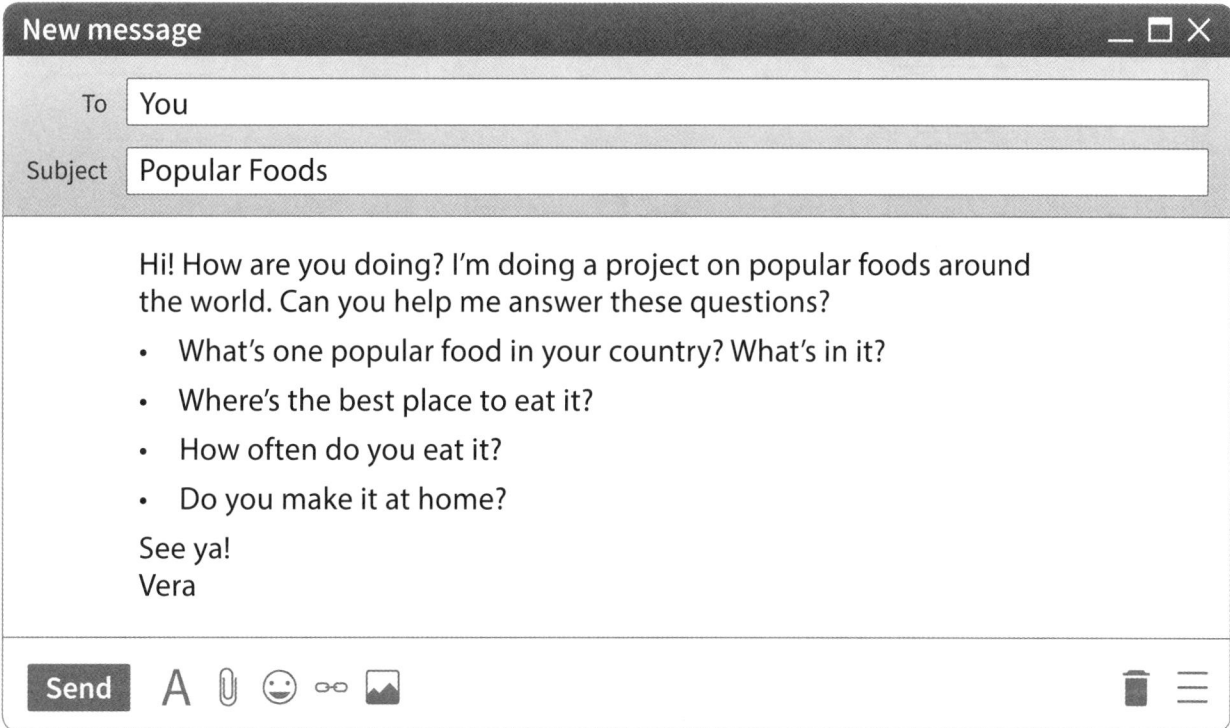

New message _ □ ✕

To | You

Subject | Popular Foods

Hi! How are you doing? I'm doing a project on popular foods around the world. Can you help me answer these questions?

- What's one popular food in your country? What's in it?
- Where's the best place to eat it?
- How often do you eat it?
- Do you make it at home?

See ya!
Vera

Send

C Write an informal email reply to Vera. Use your notes from **B**.

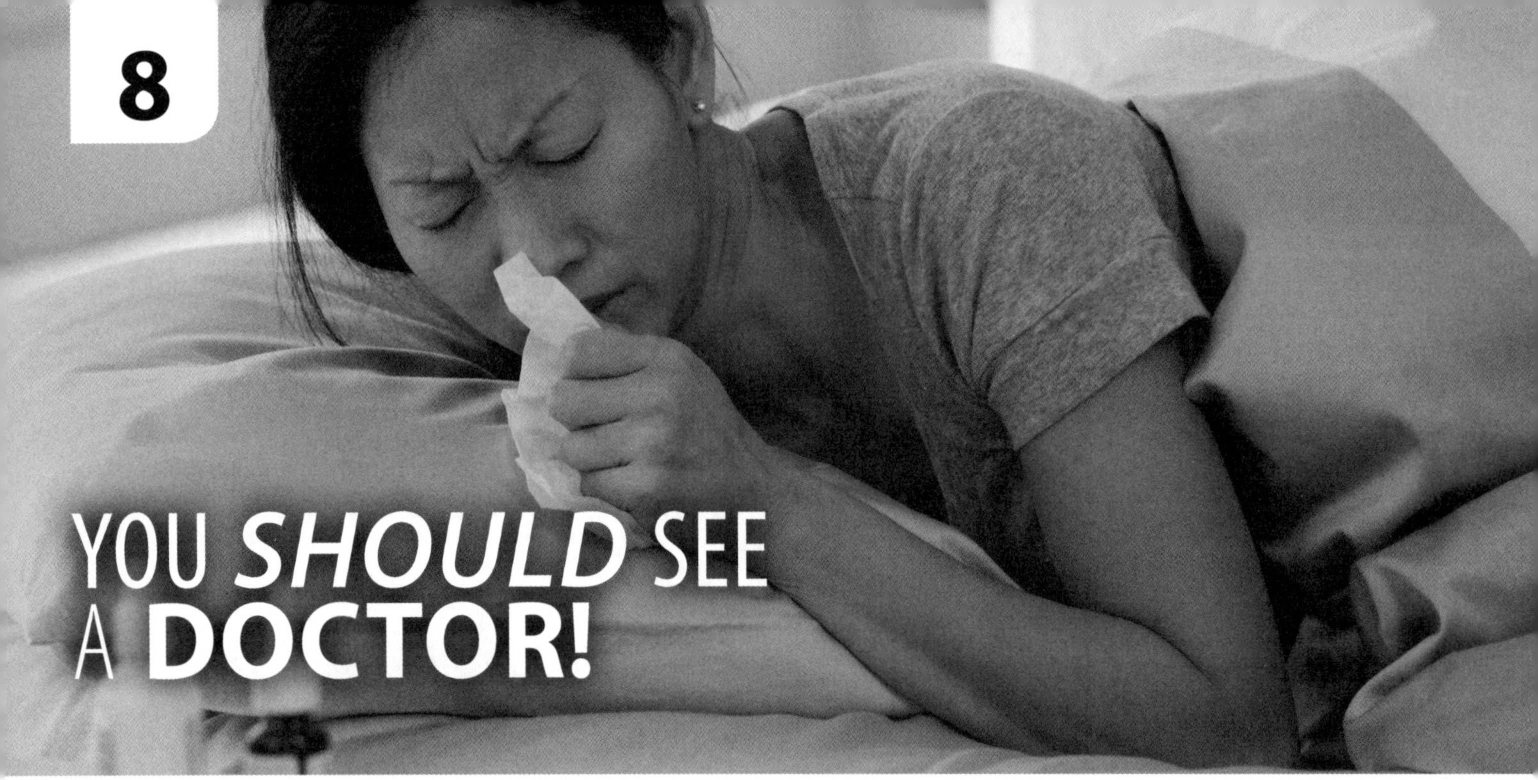

YOU *SHOULD* SEE A **DOCTOR!**

PREVIEW

A   Label the picture. Use the words in the box.

back	ear
arm	throat
leg	head
foot	knee
stomach	hand

1 _____

2 _____

3 _____

4 _____

5 _____

6 _____

7 _____

8 _____

9 _____

10 _____

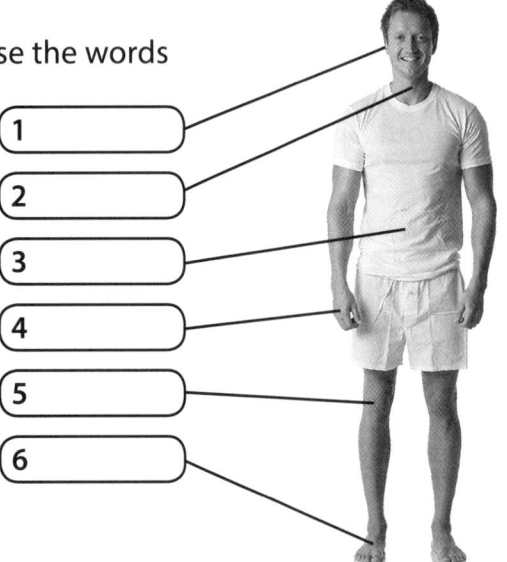
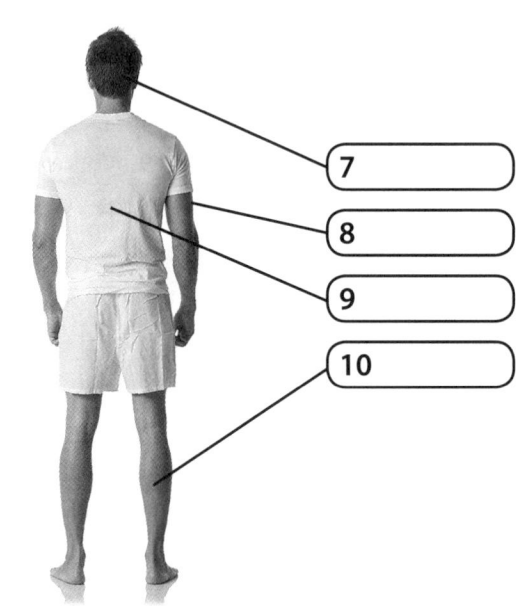

B   Unscramble the words.

1 k o e b r r   _ _ _ _ _ e n

2 e t u   c _ _

3 c d i m i n e e   _ _ _ _ i _ _ _ _

4 o s e r   _ _ _ e

5 k c i s   _ _ _ k

6 u h e g o   c _ _ _ _ _

C   Look at the pictures. Circle the correct answers.

1   **headache** / **hurt his foot**

2   sore **throat** / **back**

3   broken **arm** / **leg**

4   **hurt his knee** / **stomachache**

LANGUAGE FOCUS

A Complete the sentences and questions.

1 Jerry broke his arm. What should he _____ ?

2 May and Brian _____ stomachaches. _____ they take some medicine?

3 **Sam:** I hurt my hand. Should I go to tennis practice?

   Lucy: I don't think it's a good idea. _____ don't you stay home today?

4 Kelly doesn't feel well. She _____ go to her piano lesson today. She should rest.

5 I'm sick. What _____ I do?

B Correct one mistake in each line.

1 **Isla:** I'm have a sore throat. What should I do?

   Luka: You want rest.

2 **Chris:** My ear hurts. Should I going to school?

   Ying: No, you should staying home.

3 **Jack:** I'm feel sick.

   Kim: Why do you go to the doctor?

4 **Alan:** Lisa and Tina both have coughs. How they go to a doctor?

   Peng: Yes, they shouldn't. They can get medicine.

C Complete the conversation. Put the words in the correct order to make sentences.

Nurse: What's wrong with all of you?

Pablo: feel / I don't / a headache / well, / and I have

1 _____ .

Nurse: get / wrong / You / some / should / rest. / Kay, what's / with you

2 _____ ?

Kay: cut / knee / I / my

3 _____ .

Nurse: don't / why / here again / you / rest here? / Pat, why are you / OK,

4 _____ ?

Pat: a stomachache / I still feel / I have / really sick, and

5 _____ .

Nurse: some / Oh dear, / you / medicine / should / take

6 _____ .

Spanish biologist Pilar Bosch-Roig with a historical painting in Valencia, Spain

USING BACTERIA FOR GOOD

A Predict. Look at the picture and read the title. What's the article mainly about?

a historical painters

b harmful bacteria in paintings

c using bacteria to save paintings

When you hear the word "bacteria," what do you think of? Many people think of diseases and sickness, but there are also some good ways to use bacteria.

The beautiful paintings in Santos Juanes Church in Valencia, Italy, are old—from the 17th century—and some of the paintings had damage. For example, some parts of the paintings had a layer of white salt, while other parts had glue on them.

To clean the paintings, restorers used a special kind of bacteria. It ate the salt and glue without hurting the paintings. After 90 minutes, the restorers cleaned and dried the paintings.

B Read the article. Circle **T** for True, **F** for False, or **NG** for Not Given.

1	The paintings in Santos Juanes Church are over 900 years old.	T	F	NG
2	There was glue on some parts of the paintings.	T	F	NG
3	People used the bacteria to remove white salt on paintings.	T	F	NG
4	The special kind of bacteria can protect paintings from harmful bacteria.	T	F	NG

READING

A Look at the letters. Where do you usually see these types of letters?

a in a book   b in a magazine   c in a report

Dear Amy,

Help me! I get colds all winter—one after the other. I had a cold six weeks ago, and then another last month, and now I have a cold again! I'm tired of it! What should I do? I like school, and I don't want to stay home every time I have a cold.

Thank you,
Marissa

Dear Marissa,

I'm sorry to hear you have a cold. You should go to your doctor for some medicine. You should also drink lots of water. Eat lots of fruit and vegetables every day so you don't get more colds.

You can spread your cold to the people around you, so you should also stay home and get some rest. That way, you'll get healthy faster and other people won't get sick.

Get well soon,

Amy

Dear Amy,

My friend said traditional medicine can be very good, but I don't know anything about it. Can you give me some information? When and where did it start? How is it different from modern medicine?

Thank you,
Fabio

Dear Fabio,

I'm glad you asked. Cultures across the world, including those in the hot Amazon rainforest and cold Siberia, developed medicine and traditional cures. People started using them centuries ago.

When people go to a modern doctor, different patients often get the same medicine. For example, both you and your mom get the same cold medicine when you have a cold. But, traditional medicines vary because each patient is different. Traditional medicine experts believe that different flavors have different effects. For example, medicine that contains herbs with a sweet flavor—like licorice root—can reduce pain.

There are many things we don't understand about traditional medicine, but many people find it helpful.

Give it a try!

Amy

B EXAM PRACTICE **Answer the questions about *Ask Amy*.**

1 DETAIL What health problems does Marissa have during winter?

a colds   b stomachaches   c back pains

2 DETAIL According to Amy, it's better to drink lots of _____ to stay healthy.

a water   b soup   c fruit juice

3 PURPOSE The purpose of Amy's letter to Fabio is _____.

   a to describe the effects of different herbs

   b to introduce traditional medicine

   c to explain why traditional medicine works better than modern medicine

4 REFERENCE The word *them* in the first paragraph of Amy's reply to Fabio refers to _____.

   a various world cultures   **b** Amazon plants   **c** traditional cures

5 INFERENCE In traditional medicine, a bitter herb and a salty herb probably _____.

   a have the same result   **b** have different results   **c** don't work

C **Match.** Join the two parts of the sentences.

1 Our colds can ○	○	**a** go to the doctor.
2 Licorice root helps to ○	○	**b** treat pain.
3 To get medicine, we need to ○	○	**c** spread to people around us.

VOCABULARY

A **Complete the sentences.** Use the words in the box.

> patients   century   developed   modern   contains   pain

1 Traditional Chinese medicine _____ herbs.

2 She _____ a lunch menu for my school, so that we can have healthy meals.

3 I feel _____ in my tooth. What should I do?

4 Many _____ love this hospital because the doctors are friendly.

5 Edward Mellanby discovered Vitamin D about a _____ ago.

6 Early phones and _____ phones don't look the same.

B **Write.** Use the words in the box to write sentences with the same meaning.

> catch   recovers   look after   take

1 I have a cough, so I want to drink some medicine. _____

2 It's common to get a cold in the winter. _____

3 Parents usually take care of their children. _____

4 She's sick. I hope she gets better soon. _____

WRITING

WRITING TIP **Using *for example***

Use the term ***for example*** and give extra information to explain ideas.

A Read the information.

… the paintings had damage. **For example,** some parts of the paintings had …

comma after

The paintings had damage**, for example,** a layer of white salt and glue.

commas before and after

B Read the letter. Then complete the chart with examples of healthy habits.

> Hi,
>
> I know that eating good food, for example, fruit and vegetables, is one way to
>
> stay healthy. Can you give me some advice on other things I can do?
>
> Thanks,
>
> Ben

Healthy Habits	Examples
Exercise	
Keep clean	
Avoid junk food	

C Write a letter. Use your notes from **B** and your own ideas to write a reply to Ben.

_____

_____

_____

_____

9

I OFTEN SKATE AFTER SCHOOL

PREVIEW

A **Label the pictures.** Use the words in the box.

| practicing | studying | skating | cooking | swimming | running |

1 _____ the violin

2 _____

3 _____

4 _____

5 _____

6 _____

B **Complete the phrases.** Circle the correct answers.

1 **every** / **twice** Saturday

2 **twice** / **on** a week

3 **on** / **after** school

C **Unscramble the words.**

1 t o n e f   __ __f __ __ __

2 w y s l a a   __ __ __w __ __ __

3 m o t e s i m e s   __ __m __ __ __ __ __ __ __

4 a l y u s l u   __ __u __ __ __ __ __

LANGUAGE FOCUS

A **Look at the chart.** Answer the questions.

Saturday Schedule	Sarah	You
Morning	practice the piano	go swimming
Afternoon	skate with friends	play tennis
Evening	cook dinner three times a month	go to the beach once a month

1 It's Saturday morning. What's Sarah doing? _____.

2 It's Saturday afternoon. What's Sarah doing? _____.

3 Does Sarah ever cook on Saturday evenings? _____.

4 What do you usually do on Saturdays at 10 a.m.? _____.

5 It's Saturday afternoon. What are you doing? _____.

6 How often do you go to the beach? _____.

B **Correct one mistake in each sentence or question.**

1 I always studying after school.

2 I ever hardly exercise on Fridays.

3 Is Jack skate in the park right now?

4 What do you usually doing on weekends?

5 I rarely practicing the violin.

6 I'm exercise right now.

C **Complete the conversation.** Put the sentences in the correct order.

a _____ Oh, hi, Mom. I'm practicing the guitar.

b _____ Hmm … well, you should study some more.

c _____ Why aren't you studying? Don't you have a test tomorrow?

d ___1___ Sarah, what are you doing? What's all that noise?

e _____ I do. I'm taking a break. I already studied for a couple of hours today.

f _____ OK. After this song.

WHAT COFFEE DOES TO US

A **Skim the article.** What does *benefits* in the second paragraph mean? Check (✓) your answer.

☐ advantages   ☐ importance   ☐ problems

According to reports, over 60 percent of adults in the United States drink coffee, and they drink an average of three cups every day. Some experts believe that drinking too much coffee is a bad habit. Drinking too much coffee can cause some people to have headaches, stomachaches, and sleeping problems. Adding cream and sugar to coffee can also make it unhealthy.

However, recent studies show that drinking coffee can have benefits, too. Some studies show that drinking three to four cups of coffee a day can reduce the risk of an early death. Caffeine—a chemical in coffee—can improve brain function and make you feel better. Coffee also contains antioxidants, which help to prevent diseases.

So is coffee good for you? Researchers are still studying this, but they generally agree that a small amount of coffee each day can be healthy.

B **Read the article.** For each effect of coffee, circle **P** for positive or **N** for negative.

Coffee can …

1 cause headaches.	P	N
2 cause stomachaches.	P	N
3 improve brain function.	P	N
4 help fight diseases.	P	N

READING

A **Skim the article.** The article is mainly about what students do _____ .

a on weekends   b on most days   c on holidays

JUST A REGULAR DAY

What is your typical day like? What is it like for Americans who are 15 to 19 years old? Do you think students' answers are different in each country?

The American Time Use Survey (ATUS) is a study by the Bureau of
5 Labor Statistics. It interviewed American high school students about their average day. The ATUS shows that an average American high school student's weekday routine includes around 9 hours of sleep, 7.5 hours of studying, 4 hours of leisure activities, and 1 hour for eating. The study also shows that all students spend more time on
10 leisure activities—such as watching TV and exercising—on weekends than on weekdays.

The study found differences between male and female students. In an average day, female students spend about 8 hours on educational activities, but male students spend 30 minutes less. Male students
15 spend about 4.5 hours on leisure activities, while female students spend about 4 hours.

In most parts of the United States, teens can drive at age 16.

B **Complete the diagram.** Use information from *Just a Regular Day*.

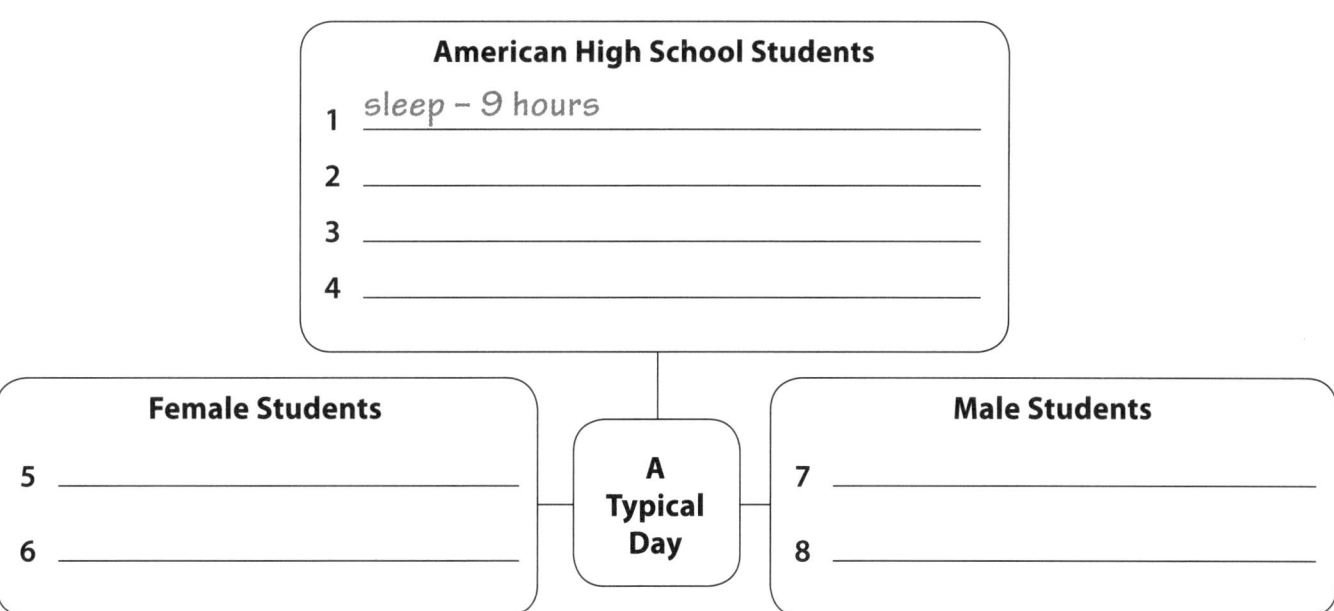

American High School Students

1 sleep – 9 hours _____

2 _____

3 _____

4 _____

Female Students

5 _____

6 _____

A Typical Day

Male Students

7 _____

8 _____

C EXAM PRACTICE **Look at the chart.** Complete the sentences.

AN AVERAGE WEEKDAY FOR A COLLEGE STUDENT IN THE UNITED STATES

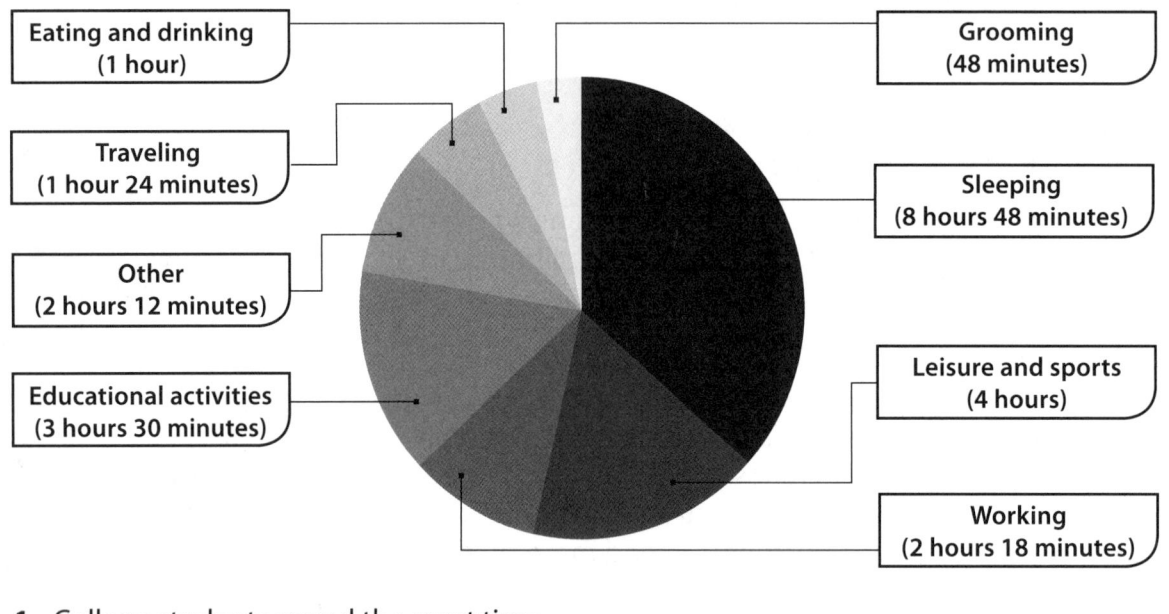

Eating and drinking
(1 hour)

Traveling
(1 hour 24 minutes)

Other
(2 hours 12 minutes)

Educational activities
(3 hours 30 minutes)

Grooming
(48 minutes)

Sleeping
(8 hours 48 minutes)

Leisure and sports
(4 hours)

Working
(2 hours 18 minutes)

1 College students spend the most time _____ .

2 College students spend the least time _____ .

3 On an average weekday, college students spend a total of _____ hours and
_____ minutes on educational activities and leisure and sports.

VOCABULARY

A **Complete the sentences.** Use the words in the box.

> bridge   choose   broken   crosses   rides   daily

1 My mom's chair was _____ , so we got her a new one.

2 In my school, we can _____ to have extra English classes.

3 The Acosta is a _____ in Florida. It _____ the St. Johns River.

4 Every morning, my grandfather reads the _____ news while eating breakfast.

5 My father _____ a motorcycle to work every day.

B **Complete the sentences.** Circle the correct answers.

1 My mom **got** / **picked** me up from school yesterday because I was sick.

2 Every morning, I **get off** / **take off** the train at Grand Central Station.

3 I **take** / **get off** the bus to work every day.

4 I **get on** / **pick** the train at Tokyo Station.

5 My flight **took** / **took off** at 12:50.

WRITING

WRITING TIP **Apostrophes**

Use an apostrophe (') and the letter **s** to show that something belongs to someone.

A **Read the information.**

The ATUS shows that an average American high school student**'s** weekday routine includes around 9 hours of sleep …

↗ **apostrophe**

For plurals ending in **s**, put the apostrophe after the **s**.

Do you think student**s'** answers are different in each country?

B **Complete the chart.** What's a typical day for high school students in your country? Write notes.

What's an average student's morning routine like?	
What do they usually do in the afternoon?	
What activities do their evenings include?	

C **Write an email.** Use your notes from **B** and your own ideas to write about a typical day for high school students in your country.

New message   _ □ ×
Hi Jack,   I'm _____. In my country, a typical student's morning routine includes   _____   _____.   In my free time, I often _____.   My hobbies _____.   What's a typical day for you, Jack?   Talk soon!

10

HOW DO YOU GET TO THE RESTAURANT?

PREVIEW

A **Complete the sentences.** Use the words in the box.

> movie theater   park   restaurant   museum   supermarket   convenience store

1 You see interesting things in a _____ , and you watch a movie in a _____ .

2 You go to a _____ to buy meat and fresh vegetables.

3 Many people go running and skateboarding in a _____ .

4 You can buy many things at a _____ . It's smaller than a supermarket, but it's usually open 24 hours a day.

5 You sit at a table and eat dinner in a _____ .

B **Complete the sentences.** Where is House **A**? Use the words in the box.

> in front of   behind   on the corner of   next to   between   across from

1 A is _____ B.

2 A is _____ B.

3 A is _____ B.

4 A is _____ B.

5 A is _____ B and C.

6 A is _____ 10th Avenue and 14th Street.

LANGUAGE FOCUS

A Match. Join the two parts of the conversation.

1 Excuse me. I'm looking for the mall. ◯ ◯ **a** That's right. It's next to the movie theater.

2 Uh … Where's Third Street? ◯ ◯ **b** No problem.

3 So, straight and then left at the corner? ◯ ◯ **c** Oh, the mall. It's on Third Street.

4 Got it. Thanks. ◯ ◯ **d** Go straight down First Avenue and turn left.

B Complete the conversation. Circle the correct answers.

Angela: Excuse me. [1] **Where / Where's** the history museum?

Chris: Oh, it's [2] **in / on** the corner of Washington Street and Elm Street.

Angela: Uh … [3] **How do / How** I get there?

Chris: Go straight down [4] **this Center / Center** Street. Then [5] **make a / make** right.

Angela: OK. Down this street and [6] **turn / turning** right?

Chris: Yes. Then go [7] **past / straight** the convenience store, and the museum is on the left.

Angela: Thank you.

C Look at the map below. Then complete the conversations. Use the words in parentheses.

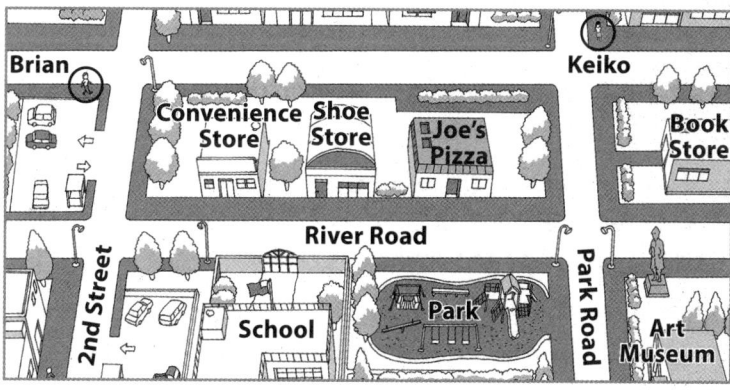

1 **Keiko:** Excuse me. How do I get to the school?

   Mark: (**straight**) _____

   (**right**) _____

   (**past**) _____

   Keiko: Thanks.

2 **Brian:** Excuse me. Can you tell me how to get to the shoe store?

   Kim: (**right**) _____

   (**left**) _____

   (**between**) _____

   Brian: Thank you.

THE REAL WORLD

A TOUR OF NEW YORK CITY

A seal at the Central Park Zoo in New York City, USA

A Scan the article. The author does NOT talk about _____.

a a zoo   **b** a beach   **c** a museum

There are so many amazing places in New York City! It's hard to decide which ones to visit, but here are a few places you can choose from.

The American Museum of Natural History is one of the world's largest natural history museums. Here, you can see models of more than 750 sea creatures. One of them is a model of a blue whale—it's almost 30 meters long! The museum also has a digging site for visitors to experience hunting for dinosaur bones.

The New York City Fire Museum gives visitors a hands-on experience. You can meet real firefighters and try on firefighters' equipment. It also has a fire engine from 1901—horses pulled it!

While visiting Central Park, don't forget the Central Park Zoo. It has many animals, including polar bears and sea lions. It also includes the Tisch Children's Zoo. At this zoo, you can touch animals, such as goats and sheep.

B Read the article. Circle **T** for True or **F** for False.

1 At the American Museum of Natural History, visitors can dig for animal bones.   **T**   **F**

2 In the article, *hands-on experience* refers to learning about something by doing it.   **T**   **F**

3 About 120 years ago, firefighters used animals as a form of transportation.   **T**   **F**

4 The Tisch Children's Zoo probably has many dangerous animals.   **T**   **F**

READING

A Scan the article. Which city was the first National Park City? _____

DEVELOPING URBAN EARTH

We can use phone apps for many things when we're outside. When we're driving, they help us to get from one place to another, or they help us find our cars and avoid heavy traffic. When we travel, we can even listen to audio tours about popular places. But Daniel
5 Raven-Ellison wants us to remember to look up from our screens so we don't miss things. He challenges everyone—including himself— to see things in new ways.

Daniel is also working to make cities greener and wilder—and more fun to live in. He wants to do this by creating National Park Cities.
10 London is the first city to receive this title. It has almost 15,000 species of animals, and there are almost as many trees as people. Londoners are making it greener, too, by growing plants in their apartments and yards.

The idea to bring nature into cities makes the environment more
15 beautiful. It is also good for our health. Studies show that nature can reduce stress and help children to learn better. So this is a win-win situation for both the people and the environment.

Daniel Raven-Ellison

B EXAM PRACTICE Answer the questions about *Developing Urban Earth*.

1 INFERENCE Daniel probably thinks people focus on _____ too much.

  a their phones   **b** their cars   **c** traveling

2 VOCABULARY In line 8, *wilder* does NOT mean _____.

  a more exciting   **b** having more wildlife   **c** more dangerous

3 DETAIL Which of the following is probably a reason why London is a National Park City?

  a It has a large number of theme parks.

  b It has many trees.

  c Most people in the city have pets.

4 DETAIL According to the article, natural areas help people _____.

  a meet others   **b** learn better   **c** exercise more often

5 REFERENCE In line 16, *this* refers to _____.

  a decreasing stress

  b having more plants and wildlife in the city

  c using technology to get from one place to another

C **Read the sentences.** Is each sentence a fact or an opinion? Write **F** for fact or **O** for opinion.

1 We should challenge ourselves to see things in new ways. _____

2 London is the first city to become a National Park City. _____

3 There are almost 15,000 species of animals in London. _____

4 Nature makes cities more beautiful. _____

VOCABULARY

A **Complete the sentences.** Use the words in the box.

> park   offers   immediately   sign   tour   traffic

1 I took the train to avoid the heavy _____ on the road.

2 I'm late! We should leave _____ .

3 The _____ says we cannot _____ our bicycles here.

4 I want to take a(n) _____ of London and see Buckingham Palace.

5 The store _____ discounts to regular customers.

B **Complete the directions.** Put the sentences in the correct order.

a _____ Then, go past the café and turn left.

b _____ First, go straight down Queen Street.

c _____ Finally, turn right. The museum is on the left.

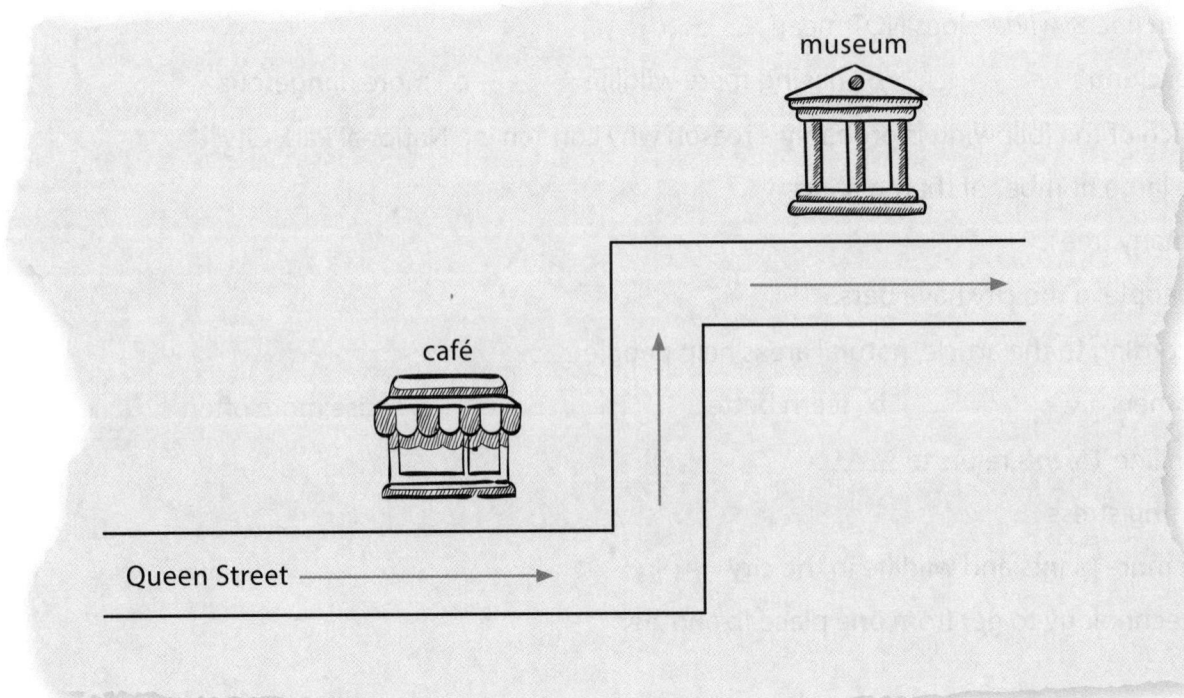

WRITING

WRITING TIP Using words to give steps

Linking words help explain the order of actions.

A Read the information.

Use the words below to help explain the order, such as when you give directions.

First / The first step is …

Second / Third

Then / After that / Later

Before / After

Finally / The last step is to …

First, take the train to Elm Street. **Then**, turn right just before the park. **After that**, turn left on Maple Street. **Finally,** go past the market.

B Complete the chart. What are some places near your school? Use your own answers.

Place Name	Description of Place

C Write a short paragraph. Use your notes from **B**. Describe the places near your school. Give directions from your school to these places.

11

WHAT WERE YOU DOING?

PREVIEW

A **Complete the sentences.** Use the words in the box.

> accident   adventures   risk   competition   experience   nervous

1 The climbers had many _____ on their way up the mountain.

2 He took a(n) _____ and started his own business.

3 She was _____ about moving to a new place.

4 She has many years of _____ in teaching.

5 She came in first at this year's dance _____.

6 He broke his arm in a traffic _____ last week.

B **Complete the phrases.** Circle the correct answers.

1 **set** / **turn** an alarm

2 **feel** / **see** an accident

3 jump **through** / **from** a height

4 **have** / **do** an experience

5 **play** / **play with** my baby sister

6 take care **with** / **of** my brother

C **Match.** Join each word or phrase to its meaning.

1 risky ○   ○ **a** get up late

2 nervous ○   ○ **b** worried

3 babysit ○   ○ **c** can be dangerous

4 sleep in ○   ○ **d** take care of children

LANGUAGE FOCUS

A **Complete the sentences.** Write the correct form of the words in parentheses.

1 I _____ (**ride**) my skateboard when I _____ (**break**) my arm.

2 My brother _____ (**jog**) when he _____ (**see**) a car accident.

3 My parents _____ (**walk**) on the beach when my mom _____ (**step**) on a jellyfish.

4 She _____ (**climb**) the mountain when she _____ (**fall**) and _____ (**cut**) her leg.

5 He _____ (**hike**) in the rainforest when he _____ (**hear**) a loud sound.

B **Correct one mistake in each sentence.**

1 I am biking when I fell over.

2 We were have a barbeque when the fireworks started.

3 I was still in bed when the phone ringing.

4 She was jogging who she saw a famous movie star!

5 I was going home when the snow start.

6 I read a letter when the bell rang.

C **Complete the conversation.** Put the sentences in the correct order.

a _____ They sure are! Then we went diving. We were looking at all these little fish when a turtle swam past us. Later we saw a baby shark, too.

b _____ Wow! I hope I can see a shark someday.

c _____ That's awesome! Dolphins are such beautiful animals.

d _____ Yeah. We saw dolphins on the boat ride out to the dive.

e _____ I sure did! I went scuba diving. It was really cool!

f _1_ I heard you had an amazing vacation.

g _____ Scuba diving? Wow! Was it your first time?

Most people forget more than 95 percent of their dreams.

STUDYING DREAMS

A Scan the article. How many kinds of dreams does the article explain? _____

Do you remember your dreams? What do they mean? Very often, you have dreams because your brain is trying to understand things that happened in the past day or two.

Do you ever dream about taking a test that you didn't study for? That's one of the most common dreams people have. Dream analysts say people with this kind of dream have a challenge in their lives. Although they are usually well prepared, they are worried that they are not ready.

Do you ever dream about running away from someone or something? That's another common dream. It could mean that you're trying to avoid a problem.

Some scientists think that dreams are just a normal part of sleep. But others think that dreams help us to understand our daily experiences and form stronger memories.

B Answer the questions about *Studying Dreams*.

1 The most suitable title for this article is _____ .

   a The Meaning of Dreams   **b** How Dreams Affect Us   **c** Good and Bad Dreams

2 Having a dream about taking a test that you didn't study for probably means _____ .

   a you don't like tests   **b** there are no challenges in your life   **c** you're worried about a challenge you've prepared for

3 When we dream about running away from something, it probably means that _____ .

   a we want to stay away from something   **b** we are thinking of ways to deal with something   **c** we can't decide on something

4 Dreams help us to _____ .

   a sleep better   **b** analyze our experiences   **c** think of creative ideas

READING

A Scan the article. At what age did Gerlinde climb her first mountain? _____

Gerlinde climbing K2, the second highest mountain in the world

UP IN THE MOUNTAINS

Gerlinde Kaltenbrunner is an amazing mountain climber. She has climbed 14 of the world's highest mountains—which are all over 8,000 meters high! Because the air is thinner, most climbers need extra oxygen to reach the tops
5 of these mountains. However, Gerlinde is the first woman to climb all 14 mountains without extra oxygen.

When Gerlinde was 13 years old, she climbed her first big mountain—Sturzhahn in Austria (2,028 meters). She became a nurse, but always had a passion for climbing. When she
10 was 32 years old, Gerlinde climbed her fifth major mountain—Nanga Parbat in Pakistan—and decided to become a full-time mountain climber.

In 2007, when Gerlinde was 37 years old, she had an accident while climbing Dhaulagiri in Nepal—the world's seventh highest mountain. She was inside
15 her tent one morning when an avalanche struck. When the avalanche stopped, it was very dark, and she didn't know where she was. She had a small knife and cut a hole in the tent. Slowly, Gerlinde managed to get out of the deep snow and to the surface.

Gerlinde recovered from the accident. "I couldn't stop climbing—this is my life," she said. "A year later I returned to the same spot. There was the most beautiful sunrise I have ever
20 seen." She climbed the 14th mountain—K2, between Pakistan and China—in 2011 and set the world record.

B Read the article. Write the letters (**a–e**) to complete the timeline below.

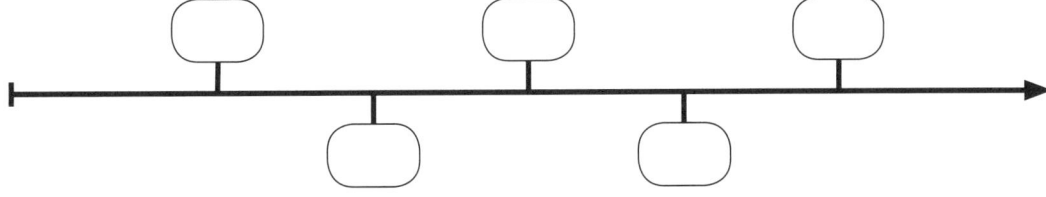

a Gerlinde started mountain climbing full-time.

b Gerlinde climbed Sturzhahn.

c Gerlinde experienced an avalanche in Dhaulagiri.

d Gerlinde set a world record.

e Gerlinde became a nurse.

C EXAM PRACTICE **Read the article.** Circle **T** for True, **F** for False, or **NG** for Not Given.

1 There's less air at the top of a mountain than at the bottom of the mountain. **T F NG**

2 Gerlinde climbed her fifth major mountain when she was a full-time mountain climber. **T F NG**

3 Gerlinde was climbing when the avalanche struck her. **T F NG**

4 Gerlinde and three other mountain climbers were hit by the avalanche. **T F NG**

5 Two men climbed all 14 mountains without extra oxygen. **T F NG**

VOCABULARY

A Complete the sentences. Use the words in the box.

> excited   hope   afraid   close   interested   wait

| Home | Blog | Photos | Contact | About Me |

Do you have a dream for the future? Some people ¹ _____ that they can find a cure for a major disease. Some people want to see wild animals up ² _____. Others can't ³ _____ to travel the world and explore new places.

Think about what you are really ⁴ _____ in. What are some things that you get ⁵ _____ about?

Don't be ⁶ _____ to follow your dreams!

B Match. Join each sentence with the meaning of the underlined word in the sentence.

1 My friend forgot her book, so we <u>shared</u> mine. ○   ○ **a** right away

2 We <u>share</u> an interest in action movies. ○   ○ **b** use together

3 Go <u>straight</u>, and the museum is on the right. ○   ○ **c** without turning

4 I'm going <u>straight</u> to the dentist after my piano lesson. ○   ○ **d** like the same thing

WRITING

WRITING TIP **Using *although***

Use ***although*** to join two short sentences with different ideas.

A Read the information.

Writers use ***although*** to tell readers they are surprised or they think something is unusual.

Although they are usually well prepared, they are worried that they are not ready.

tells us a result that is surprising
(They are well prepared, but they are still worried.)

B Complete the chart. Write notes about an adventure you had.

What was the adventure like?	
What happened on the adventure?	
What was something that was surprising at the end?	

C Write a short paragraph about an adventure you had. Use *although*.

12

WE'RE GOING TO VOLUNTEER!

PREVIEW

A Unscramble the words.

1 s e i r a   ____ _a_ ____ ____ ____ a million dollars for a project

2 a l p n   ____ _l_ ____ ____ a party

3 r a h t s   ____ _r_ ____ ____ _h_ cans

4 t p a l i s c   ____ ____ ____ _a_ ____ ____ ____ bottles

5 l e n a c   _c_ ____ ____ _a_ ____ up a room

6 t i c a r h y   ____ _h_ ____ ____ ____ ____ ____ work

B Complete the sentences. Use the words from **A.**

1 Before you leave the beach, remember to throw your _____ into the garbage can.

2 I'm going to help _____ a fair.

3 I'm going to give some books to _____ .

4 The gym is dirty—I should _____ it before the event.

5 I'm going to help recycle _____ cups and bottles from the event.

6 We're selling cakes to _____ money for new band uniforms.

C Complete the phrases. Circle the correct answers.

1 put up **decorations / trash**

2 **volunteer / raise** at a festival

3 **collect / guide** tourists around a city

LANGUAGE FOCUS

A Complete the sentences. Circle the correct answers.

1 She's **go / going** to raise money.

2 When are you **go / going to go** to the beach?

3 Are you going **making / to make** cupcakes?

4 They're going to **clean / cleaning** the beach.

5 **I'm / I** going to plan a party next month.

6 **What are / What** you going to bake?

B Complete the conversation. Put the words in the correct order to make sentences.

Peng: Let's talk about the bake sale.

Bella: OK, / going / are / it / we / have / when / to

1 _____?

Tom: month / going / have / to / next / it / We're

2 _____.

Peng: are / decorate / you / gym / going / to / the / Bella,

3 _____?

Bella: help / I am, / going / me / to / Todd's / Yes, / and

4 _____.

Tom: going / food / to / get / I'm / the

5 _____.

Peng: Great! It sounds like everything is ready!

C Look at the chart. Complete the questions and answers.

Charity Event—By Mr. Smith's Class 5 days until the event		
Next Monday	Clean the gym	Paul
Morning of the event	Put up decorations	Lee, Becky
At the event	Collect money	*Me*
After the event	Pick up trash	Jamie, Amanda

1 _____? It's in five days.

2 When's Paul going to clean the gym? _____.

3 _____? I am.

4 _____? They're going
to pick up trash after the event.

THE REAL WORLD

ON A MISSION TO RESCUE ANIMALS

Jeje uses a stone to crack open palm nuts.

A Predict. Look at the photo. What's Jeje going to do?

a eat   **b** sleep   **c** play

Poachers—people who catch animals for money—killed his mother. Then they grabbed him and took him to a big city. Brazzaville, the capital of the Republic of Congo, was far from his forest home. There, they put him in a dark room with only a little food. The poor chimpanzee became hungry and stressed. The poacher was going to sell him as a pet. But then, for some reason, the poacher changed his mind. The man reached out to the Tchimpounga Chimpanzee Rehabilitation Center, a group that saves animals. They agreed to take the little chimp in and called him Jeje.

Jeje was just a baby when the people from the center took him away. He was little for his age—he weighed only 1.8 kilograms—because he didn't have enough food when he was in Brazzaville. He was also sick when he got to the center. The staff fed him milk with a bottle. After about three months of care and love, Jeje recovered. He started to eat food and make friends with the other chimps.

B Read the article. Write the letters (**a–f**) to complete the timeline below.

a Poachers caught Jeje.

b Jeje drank milk at the center.

c People from the center took Jeje away from Brazzaville.

d Poachers took Jeje to Brazzaville.

e Jeje made friends with other chimps.

f A poacher called the center.

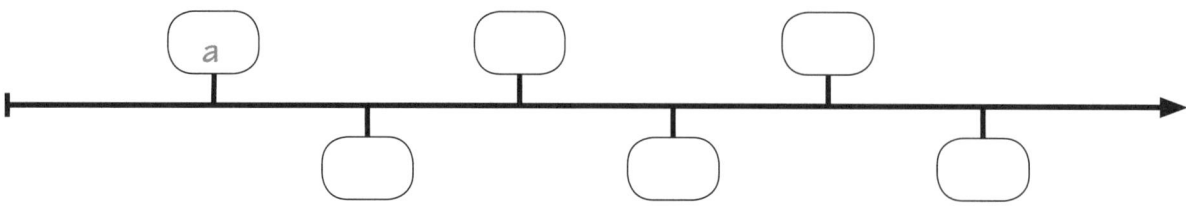

READING

A **Skim the article.** What could be another title for this article?

a   The Hungry World   b   Reducing the Earth's Population   c   Feeding the World

REDUCING WORLD HUNGER

Most people think that bacteria are bad—and some of them are. However, three high school students from Ireland found a new way to use bacteria to help grow food. The three young women—Ciara Judge,
5 Emer Hickey, and Sophie Healy-Thow—are interested in how science can help feed the Earth's growing population.

One day, Emer and her mother were in their garden and noticed something on the roots of their pea plants.
10 Emer did not know what they were, so she brought one of the plants to her science teacher. The three friends learned that pea plants have lumps on their roots containing a kind of bacteria, called diazotrophs. The bacteria help the peas grow faster, so they decided to
15 test them with other kinds of plants.

Emer Hickey, Sophie Healy-Thow, and Ciara Judge won the BT Young Scientists of the Year award in 2013.

As an experiment, they added the bacteria to barley seeds. They repeated the experiment many times. They found the plants started growing in half as much time. They also discovered the barley produced up to 30 percent more food than normal plants.

The young women say they take "a great interest in how the world works and how we can
20 help those around us." Today, they continue to work to solve the world hunger problem.

B   EXAM PRACTICE   **Read the article.** Circle **T** for True, **F** for False, or **NG** for Not Given.

1   The goal of the research is to grow more food for the world.   **T**   **F**   **NG**

2   Emer discovered the lumps on pea plants when she was in a science museum.   **T**   **F**   **NG**

3   Diazotrophs are bacteria on the lumps of pea plants' leaves.   **T**   **F**   **NG**

4   The women showed the effect of diazotrophs on the growth of barley seeds.   **T**   **F**   **NG**

5   Barley seeds taste better when we use diazotrophs to grow them.   **T**   **F**   **NG**

C Match. Join each world problem to its possible solution.

1 Millions of people do not have ○   ○ **a** Supermarkets sell "ugly" fruit and
  enough food.   vegetables at a discount.

2 We waste about one-third of ○   ○ **b** Farms use technology to grow
  the food we produce.   more food.

3 Diseases spread quickly through ○   ○ **c** We build smaller, smarter places
  the air.   to live.

4 There are not enough houses for ○   ○ **d** We use air filters to remove bacteria
  the world's population.   and viruses from the air.

VOCABULARY

A Complete the sentences. Use the words in the box.

> order   welcomed   serves   prepare   nearly   waste

1 We shouldn't _____ our money on expensive things we don't need.

2 Customers at this café _____ their food at the counter.

3 This restaurant _____ Mexican food.

4 I didn't have time to _____ lunch at home, so I bought a sandwich at the convenience store.

5 In her speech last week, the principal _____ the new class of students.

6 There were _____ a hundred volunteers at the event.

B Complete the sentences. Use the words in the box.

> leftovers   ingredients   main course   dessert

Home	Blog	Photos	Contact	About Me

Last week, the students planned a dinner to raise money for the school. First, they bought fresh

1 _____ from the supermarket. Then, they cooked the food. Guests had two choices for the

2 _____—fish or meat. For

3 _____ , the guests had cake with ice cream. The students took all of the

4 _____ home so there was no waste.

WRITING

WRITING TIP **Using *so***

Use the word ***so*** to join two sentences.

A Read the information.

Use ***so*** to say "for that reason" or to show a result. When both sentences can be independent, use a comma before ***so***.

> The bacteria help the peas grow faster. They decided to test them with other kinds of plants.

reason   **comma**

The bacteria help the peas grow faster, **so** they decided to test them with other kinds of plants.

result

B Complete the chart. Write notes about a world problem you know about.

What is the world problem?	
What causes the problem?	
What are some possible solutions to the problem?	

C Write a short report. Use your notes from **B** and your own ideas to write about a world problem and what people can do to help.

_____

_____

_____

_____

_____

_____

LANGUAGE NOTES

UNIT 1 WHAT DO YOU LIKE TO DO?

TALKING ABOUT HOBBIES (USING *LIKE TO* AND EXPRESSIONS OF FREQUENCY)	
What do you like to do after school / on weekends?	**I like to** play music.
Do you like to collect things?	**Yes**, I **do**. / **No**, I **don't**.
How often do you play soccer?	I play **once** / **twice** / **three times** a week. I **never** play soccer.
When do you do karate?	I do it **before** / **after** school on Mondays.

UNIT 2 WHAT DOES SHE LOOK LIKE?

DESCRIBING PEOPLE (USING DESCRIPTIVE ADJECTIVES)	
What does he **look like?**	He**'s tall** and he **has** short curly **hair.** He**'s medium height** and he **has** a **beard.**
What do you **look like?**	I**'m short** and I **have** brown **eyes.** I **have freckles** and I **wear glasses.** I**'m slim** and I **wear braces.**

UNIT 3 WHEN DID YOU BUY THAT SHIRT?

TALKING ABOUT SHOPPING (USING TIME ADVERBIALS)			
I like your sweater. Did you get it **recently**?	Yes, I bought it	**last**	weekend. night. week.
When did you buy your dress?	I bought it	a week	**ago.**
Are those new sneakers?	Yes, I **just** bought them	two days	**ago.**
	No, I got them	a couple of months a year	

UNIT 4 WHAT'S THE COLDEST PLACE ON EARTH?

DESCRIBING EXTREMES (USING SUPERLATIVES)		
What's **the largest** beetle in the world?	The titan beetle is **the largest** beetle.	big → the bi**gg**est
What's **the tiniest** dog in the world?	**The tiniest** dog is the Chihuahua.	pret**ty** → the prett**i**est
Some people think that Komodo Beach in Indonesia has **the most beautiful** sand in the world.		famous → the **most** famous
		good → the **best**
		bad → the **worst**
		less → the **least**

UNIT 5 ARE PARROTS SMARTER THAN PEOPLE?

MAKING COMPARISONS (USING COMPARATIVE ADJECTIVES)		
Horses are **faster than** dogs.		tall → tall**er**
I think cats are **more interesting than** fish.		bi**g** → bi**gg**er
Which are **more playful**, rabbits or turtles?	Rabbits are **more playful than** turtles, but turtles are **friendlier than** rabbits. **Both** rabbits **and** turtles are playful.	friend**ly** → friend**li**er
		intelligent → **more** intelligent
		good → **better**
		bad → **worse**

UNIT 6 I REALLY LIKE ELECTRONIC MUSIC!

GIVING AND EXPRESSING OPINIONS (USING *LIKE*)	
Do you like Imagine Dragons?	Yes, I love **them**!
Do you like Bruno Mars / Katy Perry?	Yes, I like **him** / **her**.
Do you like rap?	No, I can't stand **it**.
What kind of music **do** you **like (the) best**?	I really **like** jazz. / I **like** rock **(the) best**.
Which do you **like better**, pop **or** rock?	I **like** rock **better**.
Who do you **like better**, Ed Sheeran **or** Billie Eilish?	I like Ed Sheeran **better**.

UNIT 7 WHAT'S FOR DINNER?

EXPRESSING EXISTENCE (USING *THERE IS, THERE ARE*)			
Countable nouns		**Uncountable nouns**	
There are some plates on the table. **There aren't any** forks.		**There's some** juice on the counter. **There isn't any** ice cream in the freezer.	
Are there any apples?	Yes, **there are**. No, **there aren't**.	**Is there any** salad?	Yes, **there is**. No, **there isn't**.

UNIT 8 YOU SHOULD SEE A DOCTOR!

ASKING FOR AND GIVING ADVICE (USING MODALS)	
Maya is sick. She has a sore throat. What **should** she **do**?	She **should** stay home and rest.
I have a cough. What **should** I **do**?	You **should** take some cough medicine.
	Why don't you take some cough medicine?
Emma and Kevin both have colds. **Should** they go to a doctor?	Yes, they **should**. No, they **shouldn't**.

UNIT 9 I OFTEN SKATE AFTER SCHOOL

DESCRIBING ACTIVITIES (USING SIMPLE PRESENT AND PRESENT PROGRESSIVE)			
What are you **doing?** **Is** she **cleaning** her room?	I'm **reading** a magazine. Yes, she **is**. / No, she **isn't**.		
What do you **do** after school?	I **play** soccer **every day**. I play video games **once in a while**.		
Do you often **go** to the movies?	No, I	rarely hardly ever	**go** to the movies.

UNIT 10 HOW DO YOU GET TO THE RESTAURANT?

GIVING DIRECTIONS (USING PREPOSITIONS OF PLACE AND THE IMPERATIVE)		
Where's the museum?	It's	**behind** / **in front of** the supermarket.
		across from / **next to** the movie theater.
		between the mall **and** the park.
		on the corner of First Street **and** Main Avenue.
How do I **get to** the park?	**Go straight down** Main Street.	
	Go past the hospital.	
	Turn left / **Make a right** on First Avenue.	

UNIT 11 WHAT WERE YOU DOING?

DESCRIBING ORDER OF EVENTS (USING SIMPLE PAST AND PAST PROGRESSIVE)	
I **was skateboarding when** I **fell**.	
She **was cleaning** her room **when** I **came** home.	
We **were playing** soccer **when** the rain **started**.	
Were you **eating** when she **called**?	Yes, I **was**. / No, I **wasn't**.
What **were** you **doing** at 8 o'clock last night?	I **was studying**.

UNIT 12 WE'RE GOING TO VOLUNTEER!

DESCRIBING FUTURE PLANS (USING *GOING TO* AND EXPRESSING FUTURE TIME)	
I'm **going to volunteer** at a school event. / She's **going to sing** at the party. / They're **going to collect** food waste.	
Are you **going to come** to the party?	Yes, **I am**. / No, **I'm not**.
What's he **going to do**?	He's **going to play** music.
What are you **going to eat**?	I'm **going to eat** a sandwich.
When are you **going to go** to the mall?	I'm **going to go** there **tomorrow** / **next week**.

CREDITS

Photo Credits

Cover Beau Pilgrim; **4** Mike Hutchings/Reuters; **5** Erik Isakson/Getty Images; **6** (t) The Washington Post/Getty Images; (bl) (bc2) (br) Bioraven/Shutterstock.com; (bc1) Abeadev/Shutterstock.com; **7** Sarah Barrett; **9** SpicyTruffel/Shutterstock.com; **10** (tl) Jamie Grill/The Image Bank/Getty Images; (cl1) (cl3) (cl4) north100/Shutterstock.com; (cl2) bessyana/Shutterstock.com; (cr1) (cr4) Daria Yakovleva/Shutterstock.com; (cr2) Burakmcn/Shutterstock.com; (cr3) feepic/Shutterstock.com; **11** Barry Diomede/Alamy Stock Photo; **12** (t) AP Images/Hao qunying/Imaginechina; (b) Robyn Mackenzie/Shutterstock.com; **13** Nicolas Russell/The Image Bank/Getty Images; **14** GL Archive/Alamy Stock Photo; **16** (t) Glowimages/Getty Images; (cl1) (cl2) (cl3) Hein Nouwens/Shutterstock.com; (cl4) (cr4) Andromina/Shutterstock.com; (cr2) (cr3) Bioraven/Shutterstock.com; **18** Duy Phuong Nguyen/Alamy Stock Photo; **19** (tr) Image Source/Getty Images; (b) Robyn Mackenzie/Shutterstock.com; **20** Toltemara/Shutterstock.com; **21** (cl1) (cl2) (cl3) Andrew Rybalko/Shutterstock.com; (bl) TERPENIE/Shutterstock.com; **22** © Tom Murphy/National Geographic Image Collection; **23** Digital Vision/Thinkstock; **24** (t) Wu Swee Ong/Moment/Getty Images; (br) Dmitry Chulov/Shutterstock.com; **25** © DESIGN PICS INC/National Geographic Image Collection; **26** Rosangela Perry/Shutterstock.com; **28** Macduff Everton/The Image Bank/Getty Images; (cl1) (cl2) Julia Kutanina/Shutterstock.com; (cr1) (bl) (br) Zain Kamboh/Shutterstock.com; (cr2) Lucky Creative/Shutterstock.com; (bc) KatarinaF/Shutterstock.com; **29** (cl1) © Paul Nicklen/National Geographic Image Collection; (cl2) Simo Graells/Shutterstock.com; **30** Mark Bowler/Science Source; **31** Stefan Christmann/NPL/Minden Pictures; **34** Jason Bahr/Getty Images Entertainment/Getty Images; **35** Joseph Okpako/Redferns/Getty Images; **36** Westend61/Getty Images; **37** DEA/A. DAGLI ORTI/De Agostini/Getty Images; **38** (tl1) (tl2) (tl3) (tr1) (tr2) Aliaksandr Radzko/Shutterstock.com; (tr3) Kapreski/Shutterstock.com; **40** (t) Robert Nicholas/OJO Images/Getty Images; (cl1) Arc Tina/Shutterstock.com; (cl2) Goxy/Shutterstock.com; (cr1) tulpahn/Shutterstock.com; (cr2) Bioraven/Shutterstock.com; (cr3) Hein Nouwens/Shutterstock.com; (cr4) susannanova/Shutterstock.com; **42** Yui Mok/PA Images/Alamy Stock Photo; **43** (tr) Zou Zheng/Xinhua/Alamy Stock Photo; (bl) Habib Sajid/Shutterstock.com; **44** (t) Giraphics/Shutterstock.com; (cl) Tiger Images/Shutterstock.com; (bl) Valentyn Volkov/Shutterstock.com; (br) Billion Photos/Shutterstock.com; (cr) Karandaev/Shutterstock.com; **45** YummyBuum/Shutterstock.com; **46** (t) Ariel Skelley/Blend/Corbis; (c1) (c2) 4x6/E+/Getty Images; (bl1) Pensiri/Shutterstock.com; (bl2) Aha-Soft/Shutterstock.com; (br1) (br2) Leremy/Shutterstock.com; **47** 68/Ocean/Corbis; **48** Manuel Bruque/EPA/Shutterstock.com; **49** Gruffi/Shutterstock.com; **52** (t) © Michael Nichols/National Geographic Image Collection; (cl1) (cr1) (cr2) Leremy/Shutterstock.com; (cl2) majson/Shutterstock.com; (cl3) SoleilC/Shutterstock.com; (br) Makkuro GL/Shutterstock.com; **53** fizkes/iStock/Getty Images; **54** (t) Shuji Kobayashi/The Image Bank/Getty Images; (c) Picsfive/Shutterstock.com; **55** UpperCut Images/Alamy Stock Photo; **57** YummyBuum/Shutterstock.com; **58** Ken Seet/Cardinal/Corbis; **60** RIEGER Bertrand/hemis.fr/Alamy Stock Photo; **61** © Daniel Raven-Ellison; **62** (b) Alex Kednert/Shutterstock.com; (bc) puruan/Shutterstock.com; (br) Visual Generation/Shutterstock.com; **63** Rodin Anton/Shutterstock.com; **64** Lionel Montico/Hemis/Alamy Stock Photo; **66** Choreograph/iStock/Getty Images; **67** © Tommy Heinrich/National Geographic Image Collection; **68** Westend61/Getty Images; **70** Hero Images/Corbis; **72** Cyril Ruoso/Minden Pictures; **73** AP Images/Niall Carson; **74** Paula Solloway/Alamy Stock Photo

Art Credits

58, **59** Gaim Creative Studio

Text Credits

7 Adapted from "Addy's Mission to Save Gorillas!" by National Geographic Kids (https://www.natgeokids.com/uk/kids-club/cool-kids/general-kids-club/addy-save-mountain-gorillas/); **72** Adapted from: "Mission Animal Rescue—Chimpanzee" by Rose Davidson: National Geographic Kids, May 2015